How to Fix America

A HANDYMAN'S PLAN FOR POLITICAL REFORM

Thomas Wright Sulcer

First edition: December 2021

Cover Design and Illustrations: Natalia Junqueira | Dawn Book Design
Copyediting: Geoff Smith at geoffreypatricksmith@gmail.com
Interior formatting: Vidya and Jason of ebookpbook.com

How to Fix America

A HANDYMAN'S PLAN FOR POLITICAL REFORM

Table of Contents

Introduction

America is broken.

We know this. It's why I'm writing this and it's probably why you're reading this. We think America can be fixed and that it is worth fixing.

This book explores one way to do this.

We are aware of many of the problems: money polluting the political process, rampant inequality, a government powerless to thwart a dangerous pandemic or impending climate disaster, political polarization … and the list goes on and on. A slew of critics—politicians, political scientists, journalists, historians, reformers, military strategists, and others—have identified problems and offered solutions.

This book offers a comprehensive strategy. It identifies the major problems, how they interrelate, and shows how to fix the entire mess. No other book offers a complete solution.

I'm a handyman. Normally I work on houses, like fixing cabinet doors so they swing right, shielding PVC pipes with fire resistant sheetrock, swapping out bathroom sinks, rebuilding porches, and such.

But this project is about fixing America. I live here. I want to keep living here.

America is not going to fix itself. Lawmakers quibble over the minutiae of laws. Books and speeches obsess over polarizing hot button topics. The same talking points circulate in the media again and again. And nothing changes.

The only way to fix America is for you and me and all of us who live here and who care about our country to roll up our sleeves, to think

of ourselves as handypersons of our nation, and to fix it. Change has to come from us, from the bottom up, not from the top down.

America is like a giant house. It is made of systems and subsystems working together to bring gas for heat, electricity for lighting, and water for drinking. Like a house, its main job is to provide a safe and stable environment inside to shield us from the unpredictable and chaotic environment outside. There are plainly evident rules that can guide us in our effort to renovate our house and to renovate our nation. If we follow these rules, we'll build a good structure.

So please think of yourself as a fellow handyman or handywoman in charge of fixing our house. Think like a generalist. Think big. We live here. We care. We're the ones who suffer if it comes crashing down. We'll bring in experts when we can and apply their knowledge and insights to our good common sense.

We're the homeowners of America. Let's fix our house.

Cracks in the Foundation

WHEN INSPECTING THE HOUSE OF America, we see serious sagging, some major cracks, a tilted chimney or two, like it's one of those houses that we drive by with the overgrown lawn and moss on the roof that seems ripe for foreclosure.

A while back I repaired a porch in front of a hundred-year-old house. It was one of my toughest projects. The surface problem was that the porch floor was bouncy like a trampoline. So my first thought was, let's replace the deck. So I pulled up the decking and found that the underlying joists were warped and starting to rot, with cracks in a few places. The brick pillar supports were weak, with the mortar between the bricks beginning to crumble like sand. I could blow on the space between the bricks and the mortar would blow away. These supposedly sturdy columns were at risk of disintegrating.

So I replaced the brick pillar supports with circular concrete columns. Then I rebuilt the joists, then the flooring, then the four columns between the floor and the porch roof. It was a big job. I had advice from building inspectors and neighbors and a carpenter. But now the porch is good for another hundred years, hopefully. It's strong and sturdy.

The point, of course, is that surface problems are easy to see and usually easy to fix, but it's the deeper, harder-to-see problems lurking underneath that cause much of the fuss. If we simply fix the surface problems, it may look fixed for a while, but the problems will recur, so it isn't really fixed.

It's the same thing with America. I think many of us can see some of the surface problems. The lack of term limits in Congress. The corrupting influence of money flowing into political races. The Senate's skew such that rural less-populated states like Wyoming have greater representation than urban highly populated states like California and Florida. Gerrymandering. Political polarization. Periodic episodes of gun violence, even in schools. Opioid addiction. Haphazard foreign policy. A confused immigration approach. Inequality. Lack of healthcare. A bungled response to a pandemic. Slipshod educational policy. The precarious transition between presidents. The list goes on and on and on.

So, as handypersons looking at America, our first thought is that there are so many surface problems that we know there must be deeper issues to deal with. It's rather pointless to try to fix one or more of these surface problems without looking at what's underneath. We could replace the trampoline porch floor, and that may help for a while, but in a few years it will begin sagging again. We could repaint a porch column and it will look prettier for a while, but eventually the porch will collapse.

One lesson from my handyman work is this: do only one thing at a time. Sounds obvious, right? But trying to do two things at once is how accidents can happen. Case in point: I was installing a sheetrock panel on a kitchen ceiling. Walking down the ladder, the one thing I should have been doing was watching each step as I descended, but I was thinking about the next piece of sheetrock. I was trying to do two things at once. I thought I was at the bottom step but surprise, there was one more. So I fell back on the kitchen floor with the ladder on top of me. Luckily, I didn't get hurt.

So to fix America, let's look at one problem at a time. Let's begin by looking at one of the more serious problems first. I don't think it's the ultimate underlying problem, but it is a serious one.

America is polarized into two rival camps—Democratic and Republican—and there is little agreement between them. Each party thinks differently. Each follows its own media. It's as if the country is on the verge of a civil war.

Why would a nation, which is supposed to be one nation, divide itself into two opposing camps? It's as if a whole house decided to cleave itself in two.

It happened not because of any external problems, like war or the threat of war, or economic calamity, or a mass influx of new people who speak a different language. There have been no earthquakes to shake it into two halves. There was a pandemic but the division happened years before the virus struck.

But the United States is an old house, and older houses have more problems. Moisture can rot wood. Door hinges shake loose. If we estimate America's age based on the adoption of the Constitution, it's 240 years old.

So I think we need to look at the Constitution since it's like the framework of our house. It is the legal underpinning of our system of government that describes the parts of government and how they relate to each other. Laws and rulings are built on top of this foundation, like the walls of a house are built on its foundation.

When a problem develops as serious as a house splitting into two halves, without an easy-to-spot cause, we should not be looking at particular walls or people in the house or whether the roof is leaking.

We should be looking at the Constitution.

The Constitution isn't something that is sacred or perfect or inspired by divine wisdom. It's basically a set of laws underneath the laws.

Our Constitution was built to be adapted with amendments, though the process of passing amendments is difficult. It's as if the foundation of the house could adjust to shifting conditions, like adjustable blueprints that allow new rooms to be added or ceiling heights to be adjusted.

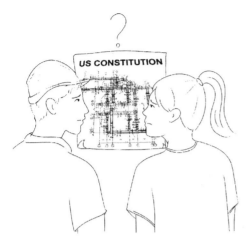

But our Constitution has not been adapting itself well to changing conditions. Though there have been some positive amendments, the basic structure is rather stubborn, like it's still mostly an eighteenth-century Constitution while we're living in the twenty-first century.

So at this point, let's start thinking about what some of the underlying problems might be.

My first thought is that the country is divided into two parties. In a two-party system, our choices are limited. It's either us or them. This or that. There are no third or fourth or fifth or sixth choices. It's like shopping in a supermarket for soda but there are only two choices: Coke or Pepsi. No Sprite. No Doctor Pepper. No Snapple. No root beer. With politics limited to only two choices, it seems likely that the public will gravitate to two ways of thinking.

But when we examine the Constitution, we see that it doesn't explicitly require two parties. A likely guess, then, is that the rules governing elections cause there to be only two parties. Still, the Constitution doesn't talk much about election rules. Rather, the Framers left it up to the states to decide how to run elections.

As handypersons on the jobsite America, we know how joists and studs work. Joists are the horizontal boards running beneath ceilings and studs are the vertical boards inside walls. Every joist and stud should be sixteen inches away from the next one. Knowing this, it's easy to find studs hidden behind walls when attaching a cabinet, for example. Just as joists and studs determine the structural integrity of a floor or a wall, election rules determine how many parties emerge.

Back in the eighteenth century, almost all states chose a winner-take-all arrangement for electing representatives and the president. It is sometimes called the first-past-the-post system because whichever candidate, like in a horse race, gets past the post of 50% of the votes, gets all of the votes. They're first. They win everything, even the votes of the people who didn't vote for them. It seems fair, right? The winner won, so the winner takes all, right? Today 48 states use the winner-take-all system.

As handypersons, we know that we don't know everything about houses, which is why we consult construction engineers, plumbers, electricians, architects, and so forth. So when we're trying to fix America, we consult political scientists and constitutional scholars and academics who study politics.

What political scientists know today, but what the Framers didn't know back then, is that the winner-take-all approach produces only two parties. When we look at Congress, elected officials are either Democratic or Republican. There are no other parties except for a rare independent. When we vote, there are spaces on the ballot for third and fourth and fifth parties, and sometimes there are even candidates from these parties, but these candidates never seem to get elected.

What happens is that, over time, the winner-take-all system teaches voters to vote for a candidate from one of the two main parties. To vote for a third or fourth or fifth likely candidate is not only wasting one's vote, but it's likely to help the candidate that one likes the least.

Let me explain. Suppose there are three candidates: A, B, and C. Suppose we like candidate C. They're closest to our interests. B is acceptable to us but we don't want A. If we vote for C, we're taking away a vote for B, a vote that B would have gotten, hurting B. Since there will be only one winner in the winner-take-all arrangement, then A is more likely to win if we vote for C. In effect, voting for C helps elect A, which is what we didn't want.

Voters aren't stupid. We learn that if we don't vote for one of the two mainstream candidates, A or B, that we'll help elect the person that we didn't want to win.

Let's view this from another perspective. As a voting system, winner-take-all does a substandard job of representing what voters want. Who does it represent? The winners. Who doesn't it represent? The losers. Though the losers lost, shouldn't they still get some representation in the legislature? So at least their viewpoints and arguments and facts get heard in the legislative wrangling? Yes, they should.

This gets at the core idea of a representative government. The simple idea, of course, is that representatives should represent the people. We the people are so numerous that it doesn't make sense for us to vote on every issue or try to grapple with the details of governing, so we choose a small group of people, a subset of us, to represent our views in the government.

What's important is that the representatives should mirror the public. The problem with winner-take-all is that it's a bad mirror. It only reflects the winners. It doesn't reflect the losers. The views of the public are distorted in the legislature.

So as fixes go, this one is fairly straightforward.

A better system is proportional representation. It works as follows: Suppose 15% of the public wants A, 40% wants B, and 45% wants C. That's what we want. The idea of proportional representation is that these percentages are reflected in the legislature, so that 15% of the legislators favor A, 40% favor B, and 45% favor C. In this case, the representatives faithfully represent the public. It's a better mirror.

With proportional representation, debates within the legislature are more likely to be lively and thoughtful because different views are represented. The principle of majority rule will still be in effect, so when the legislature votes on any given proposition, the majority will still prevail. But with different parties in the legislature, the legislators will probably have to compromise when making laws. That's good. When the legislature acts, it is much more likely to reflect what the public really wants.

As noted earlier, the Constitution does not explicitly require the winner-take-all system to elect congresspersons; it said nothing, so it is essentially an error of omission. But the Constitution does require the winner-take-all arrangement when electing presidents through the convoluted voting system called the Electoral College. If a candidate for president wins a majority of votes within a state, they win the entire state. It's as if the persons within a state who voted for the losing candidate didn't even vote. Their votes didn't count. Their votes are essentially discarded from the national tally.

The flawed Electoral College system sometimes allows a presidential candidate who loses the popular vote to win the presidency. This happens when one candidate wins a slight majority in enough states to counterbalance the huge majority of votes for their opponent in a few states. This has happened five times in the past. It is a clear violation of the principle of majority rule. The nation elects a president that most people didn't want.

Further, the flawed Electoral College system disenfranchises many voters. Consider that many states are heavily Democratic or Republican, based on what we know from past elections. So voters in these firmly blue or firmly red states know that their vote is unlikely to affect the outcome of a presidential election. Massachusetts votes Democratic. Alabama votes Republican. So why vote when a voter knows in advance who will win their state? This is how the Electoral College disenfranchises voters in solidly blue or solidly red states. Their votes don't really count, while the voters in so-called swing states, in which the proportion of voters for each of the two parties is approximately equal, count disproportionately. Swing state voters have more power than voters from solid-color states.

Though the Constitution's Framers got many things right, they goofed when it came to specifying election rules. They didn't understand how leaving such rules up to the states would let them choose the flawed winner-take-all system, and how that would lead, over time, to a polarizing two-party system. So a fix should be to switch from winner-take-all to proportional representation, which would require an amendment to the Constitution.

Since there are other problems with the Constitution, we will get around to these fixes since there are others still to come. And the fixes must be handled in a coordinated way.

We're just getting started. It's like we're just lifting the floorboards of the porch.

As handypersons of America, we should try to fix things based on sound building principles. We know the walls on the first floor have to be strong enough to support the weight of the second floor. We know that removing a beam requires an understanding of the weight above it. When we see a failure to specify a multiparty arrangement, it is like a load-bearing wall made of particle board. Particle board is wood chips glued together with resin and it isn't as strong as hardwood lumber. It's suitable for cabinets but not for walls. To me, it seems like parts of our Constitution are made from particle board.

Switching from winner-take-all to proportional representation is like trying to replace a weak load-bearing wall with a stronger one. Such a change will affect other structures in the house.

How to Build a Strong House

SO LET'S IDENTIFY THE BASIC principles of a strong nation. These include:

- **Self-rule**. We the people rule ourselves.
- **Majority rule**. Decisions are made by the majority. This is good because decisions will probably benefit the most people, not just a sliver of the public.
- **Representative government**. Legislators represent the public. They're accountable to voters. They *mirror* the people, like I said.
- **One person, one vote**. A person's vote has the same influence weight as anyone else's, with the basic underlying principle being an equality of political power, so that swing state voters don't have more political clout than voters from solid-color states.
- **Competitive elections**. Candidates running for office compete on a level playing field so that no candidate has an unfair advantage.
- **National self-determination**. Our own government determines our foreign policy, not foreign governments or dictators or multinational corporations or foreign lobbyists.
- **Rotation of offices.** In the ancient Roman Republic, officials would not linger in one office but would rotate to other offices. The continual shuffling of officials meant that each one got valuable experience by learning the mechanics of each position. Further, the shuffling lessened the probability that a corrupt official could wedge themselves into a cushy and corrupt arrangement and keep it hidden.

These are good principles. They're common sense. These design guidelines are like those guiding the building of a house. For example, lower-level structures should be stronger and sturdier than the upper-level structures because they bear more weight. So foundations are made of reinforced concrete, first floor walls are made of reinforced studs, and the top floors are made of plywood. We have to account for things that might happen. Architects use terms like *live load* to describe things like heavy furniture and people and snow on the roof that might be added to the house, to make it heavier, and wind that might push the house sideways. The structure has to be strong enough to withstand these forces. The structure should be adaptable, so if new wiring or heating technologies become available in the future, it is easy to accommodate such changes without having to knock down walls.

If we examine our current political system in light of these basic principles, these principles sometimes hold, and sometimes they don't. It is as if our national house has gotten some things right but that there are serious structural flaws.

Consider that most elections for Congress aren't really competitive. Once a congressperson gets in office, there's a 90% or greater likelihood that they will keep getting reelected every two years. Some congresspersons stay in office for ten, twenty, sometimes thirty years. This can sometimes be good if they become more experienced in governing. But if they're going to get reelected no matter what, they don't really need to listen to what we want. They're no longer accountable to us.

In only a few cases, when a congressional seat opens up, then the next election for their seat becomes competitive. There is a choice, although as noted previously, it's limited to two mainstream candidates. When a seat opens up, neither candidate has the advantage of incumbency. So the system isn't totally broken.

But in subsequent elections after a competitive election, the incumbent will most likely win because they have several advantages. First, they have greater access to campaign cash. This is part of a self-fulfilling cycle since if incumbent politicians are presumed to win reelection, then donors are more likely to donate to their campaigns, and the cycle repeats. Some incumbent candidates have a six-to-one advantage in terms of campaign funding. An incumbent congressperson needs money for advertising and campaigning, so well-heeled check writers can have a powerful influence over the congressperson compared to the voters. This distortion works against good representation.

A second unfair advantage is that incumbents get free mailings called franking privileges. These are supposed to help congresspersons communicate with their constituents, but in practice, they are thinly veiled advertisements. Challengers don't have similar free mailings.

A general problem that undercuts competitive elections is that incumbent politicians, wanting to get reelected, can make rules to improve their chances. They have power. They write the rules. So they can write rules to give themselves an unfair advantage at the ballot box. It's as if incumbent politicians have a monopoly of sorts.

It's like shopping for sheetrock but there's only one hardware store close by. We're steered into buying from the *incumbent politicians* store. The other store of *challenger politicians* is farther away and the roads to get there are full of potholes, so we buy from the closer store even if it charges higher prices.

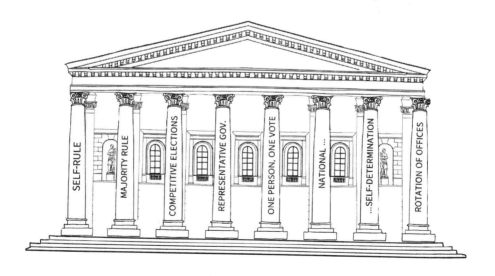

An egregious example of the unfair power of incumbency is when a president is up for reelection. They control some of the machinery of the federal government. It is tempting to abuse this machinery to get an unfair advantage if they run for a second term. This is what the Watergate scandal was about: In 1972 President Nixon, the incumbent running for reelection, hired political operatives to break into the opposing party's campaign headquarters to search for dirt on his opponent. He won reelection, but he was caught and forced to resign from office. In 2020 incumbent President Trump tried to sabotage the US Post Office. When many voters, trying to keep safe during a pandemic, opted to vote by mail, Trump installed a crony to head the post office who dismantled many of the mail-sorting machines to slow down the delivery of absentee ballots.

When a president runs for reelection, and if the contest is fair, then their chance of winning should be about 50-50. It's the highest office in the land. Plenty of highly capable politicians vie for this office. But looking at the historical record, an incumbent president wins reelection about two-thirds of the time, which suggests that these elections are not truly competitive. Who gets hurt by this lack of competition? We do.

You've probably heard these two words before: term limits. Is it likely that incumbent politicians will vote to impose term limits on themselves? Probably not. They like their jobs. They get a sumptuous salary. They vote for generous benefits and pensions and healthcare coverage for themselves. They have power and want to keep it. So naturally neither party will push for term limits, particularly when their party has the majority.

Term limits should be built into the Constitution in order to keep elections competitive. Ideally, for elections to the House of Representatives, there should be no politicians running for reelection so no candidate would have the unfair advantage of incumbency. Though there is a two-term limit for the presidency limiting them to eight years in office, even that is problematic, since presidents are tempted to abuse their authority to win reelection to their second term. Ideally, presidents should only be in office for one term.

A well understood way that incumbent politicians can rig the rules to make reelection easier is gerrymandering. State politicians from the same party draw the congressional districts in such a way as to make it easier for their party's congressional candidates to get reelected. By drawing these maps, it is as if political parties were choosing their voters, rather than voters choosing their representatives.

Like the constitutional flaws of winner-take-all and the two-party system, gerrymandering is one more example where the Constitution fails by not specifying how elections should be held. It is one more flaw of omission. The Constitution left it up to the states, and the state governments did a bad job by allowing and fostering gerrymandering. Both parties do it. It's legalized corruption. And it's been around since the 1820s—and even earlier by some accounts.

So far, looking at our handyman fixer-upper, we've identified two serious flaws that, by themselves, require constitutional amendments. But there are even deeper flaws that affect the entire structure and are more insidious because they're hiding in plain sight.

I remember trying to fix that porch. My initial inspection missed that much of the structure that had to

Keep the Good Stuff, Fix the Flaws

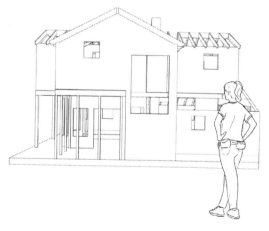

be rebuilt. So I was able to keep the roof and steps, but I had to replace the concrete footers and joists and columns and railings. That's a general handyman principle: keep the good stuff, and fix the flaws.

So far I've tried to identify some major flaws regarding election rules and the lack of term limits. If we fix those two flaws, will the house of America still stand?

I think the flaws are deeper.

Remember, a democracy is based on the notion of self-rule in that we rule ourselves. Even the word *democracy* is from the roots *demos*, or "the people," and *cracy*, or "rule."

Suppose we fixed the election rules and imposed term limits. Would we the people still participate in the process of ruling ourselves? What's to keep us from getting absorbed in entertainment, attending to business and shopping, and getting distracted in the day-to-day experience of chores and family and school and hobbies and such?

My sense is that the problems are deeper because the connection between the people and the government is weak and tentative, and I see this as one of the underlying structural problems with the United States.

How to Be Good Homeowners

LET ME IDENTIFY WHAT I see as one of the most dangerous structural flaws with our system of government. It is one more failure of omission.

Citizenship.

The original Constitution didn't specify who a citizen was or what citizenship was all about.

If the idea of a good nation is self-rule—that is, we the people ruling ourselves and being in charge of our own destiny—then clearly the Constitution should specify how we should rule ourselves, and what our role should be in doing this self-ruling.

The Constitution should answer these questions: What is our role as a citizen? How do we go about the task of being citizens? What are the duties and privileges of citizenship? What if some people don't want to or can't be citizens?

But the Constitution rarely addresses these questions.

To be fair, there have been some positive constitutional developments regarding citizenship. During our history, the question of who is a citizen has expanded. First, it was only adult white males with property. Then white male adults. Then all adult males. Then women. This expansion is good. It is one of

the few examples where the Constitution has adapted itself positively over the past twenty-four decades.

But the Framers did not specify how we the people were supposed to rule ourselves. They set forth a system of government with various branches, including Congress, the presidency, and the judiciary, but they left out the most important part: us. It's a huge error of omission. In failing to specify our role as citizens, the Framers seriously neglected us.

Their neglect was not total, however, since they specified in the Bill of Rights a set of important personal protections. We have the power to assemble. We have the freedom of speech and religion. We can not be compelled to testify against ourselves, and so forth, and these rights are extremely valuable.

But in the matter of how we should go about being citizens, including our responsibilities and privileges, there is little guidance. It is a void. It's almost as if the Framers did not really want us to be active citizens, as if we're an afterthought, an unfortunate guest at a party who arrives without a nametag at their table. It's as if citizens show up at the construction site, but there are no parking places for our trucks.

To rule collectively, together, and rule ourselves, we must act as citizens, real citizens, who actively participate in running our nation.

I suppose most of us think we're citizens. We have passports. We have certain privileges and rights. We can vote. We call ourselves citizens.

But most of us participate only minimally in the political process. About half of us don't bother to vote for president every four years. We rarely meet with our representatives. Most of us don't even know our representatives' names or their positions on various issues.

A better description of us is that we're more like consumers. We live here. We work here. We belong. We have certain rights and freedoms.

It's like we've trusted the political process to run itself. It's like we're tenants in a big house. Like we're the employees and not the owners of the construction company that we work for. We get to live here but we don't own the house. We don't get to make many decisions about how our house is run. We let politicians make these decisions for us, and they don't always have our best interests at heart.

So let's clarify what being a real citizen is all about. A real citizen...

- Keeps themselves informed about current events
- Meets with fellow citizens from time to time as a citizen
- Thinks like a citizen by paying attention to issues
- Makes informed guesses about public policy
- Votes
- Respects reality
- Talks about political issues with words, not fists
- Settles disputes in a reasonable manner
- Obeys the law
- Pays taxes
- Tells the truth
- Respects the rights of other people

There's an important aspect of citizenship that I will address soon, but for now, let me elaborate on the concept of rights. That needs a bit of explaining. I think most people have a general sense of what they're about, but it's such an important concept that clarification can be helpful.

In house building, the concept of gravity is central. Things get pulled vertically to the Earth. That's why we build walls straight up that are plumb, at a ninety degree angle to the Earth, so that the walls push directly upward and carry the weight with the greatest efficiency.

Like the concept of gravity, the concept of rights is central to the building of political systems. Simply, a right is a power to do something in the future that people agree about in the present. I can do something. You can do something. Everybody agrees in the present that we can do those things in the future.

This before-we-act agreement is fundamental to everybody's freedom. It means we can do all sorts of things, knowing in advance that we can do them and that when we do, we won't be punished afterward for having done them.

A right is like a bubble of future action that surrounds us. We can walk on the sidewalk. We can wave our arms. We can hop.

The idea of a good society is to expand these bubbles of future action as far as possible, provided that they don't bump into the bubbles of other people. This expands everybody's freedom. It helps us all work together in a coordinated fashion with a minimum of violence and harm.

We can think of the space between bubbles as a custom or as a law. For example, on a two-way road, you can drive on one side, and oncoming traffic can drive on the other side, and the double yellow line down the road is like the law saying stay on your side of the street. It makes sense. Drivers can travel quickly with few collisions. It's safer.

The idea of a good society is to expand our bubbles of possible future action as far as possible provided that they don't interfere with the rights of others.

What's important, as I said, is that people agree in advance about these rights. Drivers should know to keep to their side of the road. The idea of keeping to your side needs to be in the brains of all drivers. If some drivers do not follow these rules, there will be crashes. All it takes is for one driver to disobey and a head-on collision could result, diminishing everybody's freedom and snarling traffic.

Though the concept of rights is powerful and freeing, it is also fragile. It doesn't take much for the system to fall apart if some people disagree.

This concept is the fundamental building block for law, and it can be built into a comprehensive legal system with other rights. For example, a right can be built upon another right, such as a citizen having the right to vote being built on having citizenship. Some rights are dependent on other rights: if I buy a ticket to ride on a train, that right might be contingent upon other rights, such as the right of the railroad service to regulate behavior, like not allowing riders to put their feet up on chairs. Though the system of rights can be complex, the underlying principle is simple.

Citizenship is about respecting these rights. We value our rights and we respect the rights of others. We want our bubbles of possible future action to be as large as possible since it means that we can do more things, go to more places, learn more skills, and have more opportunities to enjoy living. Further, we want our fellow humans to enjoy similarly large bubbles of future action so they too can enjoy life, and as they become more powerful, there are more ways that they can help us. Citizenship is about respecting the boundaries between these rights as well, so that our actions don't interfere with the actions of others, and defining these boundaries is what law and government and constitutions are all about.

Citizenship is, in a sense, a bundle of political rights. It's like a framework that numerous specific rights are built upon, as if it's a right to have rights, such as the right to vote, the right to hold office, the right to receive fair and equal treatment under the law, and so forth.

Yet citizenship is more than simply rights because it implies privileges and responsibilities. It should not be a merely passive relation but an active one. Citizens should participate actively in the political process. It's what democracy is all about: we the people rule ourselves.

So a part of understanding the problem with America is getting a firm understanding of what citizenship should be. A real citizen does what real citizens do: we vote, we serve on juries or in the military if summoned, we pay attention to current events, we form opinions about public issues, we read newspapers, we have discussions with other citizens about what to do, and we respect the rights of fellow citizens to do similarly.

Real citizens are connected with our representatives. We can learn from our representatives about what is happening in the government and what issues confront them, and our representatives, in turn, can find out what we want. It should be a two-way communication. We say what we want, and representatives listen. Representatives tell us about the political constraints, and we listen. This back-and-forth communication continues to enlighten both the citizen and the representative.

Being a real citizen requires a certain mindset that is characterized by an openness to new ideas, a willingness to learn, a respect for facts and for how various facts relate to each other, and an ability to guess what might happen in the future. It requires a level of mental skill to connect facts and form an opinion about the real world. Such citizens value what is good for themselves and, by extension, for the wider community, in wider and wider spaces, and in longer and longer time frames. We compare alternatives and choose what we think is the best one. We might not guess correctly, but we must be able to guess what we think is the best course of action. It helps if we can communicate with other citizens about why we think that a certain course of action is best, and have the presence of mind to listen to counterarguments.

Today in America there are few real citizens like this. Because of political polarization, people have gravitated toward two mutually opposed media ecosystems and developed incompatible orientations about public life. We segregate ourselves geographically, so our neighbors tend to think like us. It is as if each of the two mainstream political parties has its own set of facts and beliefs and values. The Republican Party bubble, at present, seems to be about respect for religion, for individual freedom, and for unregulated free enterprise. The Democratic Party bubble seems to be about respect for science, for group freedom, and for business regulation. In 2020 and 2021, each side had a different strategy for how to deal with the contagious and deadly COVID-19 virus; one side believed in wearing masks while the other side didn't, which led to a confused response to a dangerous disease.

SCIENCE
GROUP FREEDOM
REGULATION OF BUSINESS
CNN AND MSNBC

RELIGION
INDIVIDUAL FREEDOM
UNREGULATED BUSINESS
FOX NEWS

Political polarization, caused by the flawed two-party system, makes it difficult for people from different viewpoints to have reasoned discussions about what is happening. It is almost as if bringing up any political subject with another person violates an unwritten rule about keeping one's political views to oneself. So at parties, at the office, in polite company, people self-censor, and evade talking about any political subject lest it degenerate into a heated argument that cuts short any chance of a productive future relationship.

This is dysfunctional. It is bad. We need to be able to talk with each other about politics. This is how we can learn what is going on. But this doesn't happen, and it furthers a tendency for people to live in separate political bubbles.

How do we fix things so people behave and think like real citizens? It is clear that the current Constitution fails in this regard, since it doesn't specify what citizenship is, and it doesn't say what the privileges and duties of citizenship are.

So to fix this, the Constitution should specify that citizenship means ...

- **Active participation in politics.** For example, every four months, we meet with other citizens, for at least a half-hour, to keep informed about public policy.
- **Voting.** This should be required. Currently it is optional.
- **Jury duty.** If a citizen is summoned for jury duty, then they should try to do an adequate job of being a juror. They listen to arguments and counterarguments, form opinions, respect facts, and make a reasonable decision about guilt or innocence.
- **Paying taxes.** The government, of course, cannot do its job without payments from citizens. Paying taxes is important because it gives us a firm feeling that we own our government collectively. It's our government. We bought it with our tax payments. This means, in part, doing away with automatic systems that bypass a citizen's choice of whether to pay taxes, such as when taxing authorities collect taxes directly from our employer, bypassing us.
- **Military service.** If we are summoned, then it is vital that we do, in fact, serve in the military. This is highly important for later fixes regarding national self-determination. Briefly, the government needs to know, when it jostles with other states in the international world, about which of its members are in and which are

out if a conflict happens. Government should not have to guess whether we will choose to support a war. If a person is a citizen, then we promise to fight for our nation if we have to. It hurts everybody if the government decides that it has to fight a war and nobody shows up. Further, it means that if a citizen promises to fight but doesn't, that such a person can be rightly punished for abandoning their earlier promise. Most likely Congress will make rules to punish people who decide before an impending war to sever their bonds of citizenship.

- **Thinking like a citizen.** A citizen strives to be open-minded, to respect reality, and to value facts and the workings of cause-and-effect. We have a basic education. We can think and act and talk like a citizen. We can argue constructively without discussions degenerating into name-calling or personal attacks. It means being ready to acquiesce to the will of the majority. It means keeping oneself informed about current events. It means valuing the democratic process itself, including free and fair elections, majority rule, voting, rights, and representative government.
- **Obeying the law.** If a person violates the rights of other people, or steals, or cheats on their taxes, or does other criminal activity, then they're not worthy of being a citizen. They've demonstrated by their conduct that they are not to be trusted with political power.

There is one key aspect of citizenship that I haven't mentioned before. It is a key responsibility. It is ...

- **Protecting fellow citizens.** We look out for each other if the government becomes abusive to one of us.

This deserves further explanation.

There is always a danger, in any society, of the government abusing its power to hurt citizens. The way that a good society should work is that we surrender much of our power to the government, and entrust it with the authority to settle disputes impartially and fairly according to laws that are hopefully good. Still, this gives the government tremendous power over us. It can put us to death. It can imprison us. It can strip us of our money and livelihoods. It can impose harsh regulations on our businesses.

Accordingly, a proper duty of every citizen should be to look out for the health and welfare of our fellow citizens, and to watch how the government treats people, and to complain loudly, through law, if we think that the government has overstepped its authority and unfairly harmed one of us.

That means me looking out for you, and you looking out for me. We protect each other with our collective political power. It is the proper way to protect each other, by paying attention, by following what's going on, and if abuse happens, we use words and logic and arguments to end the abuse through legal procedures without using violence.

Accordingly, we don't use guns to protect ourselves from abuse by the government. That's a losing battle. The government has exponentially more guns than we could possibly gather. They have highly trained officers and they can coordinate their various agencies easily to overpower even the most stalwart opponent. That's the government's job: to maintain law and order. They have a legal monopoly of force over a given geographic area. Not surprisingly, there have been no instances in the past where a heavily armed individual, or even a group of heavily armed individuals, held out against the might of the government, although there have been outlaws and criminal gangs that evaded capture by hiding and running.

So gun ownership as a means of self-protection is badly misguided. Instead we must protect ourselves by working together as citizens to watch out for each other's safety. This is how we protect ourselves: with words, with the law, with lawyers, and by being vigilant.

The idea of living in a civil society is that we band together for mutual protection. We give up our rights of self-defense to the law and to police and to the government because these entities are more likely to be an impartial judge when we become involved in disputes. It is like a contract between us and the state: the state must protect us from criminals and from foreign armies and resolve our disputes with neighbors, and we obey the law. It is an extremely beneficial relationship.

It is freeing in that we don't have to arm ourselves or build castle walls around our houses or drive around in a Sherman tank because if there is trouble, we can call 911 and have trained police officers show up to resolve the issue. If we have a dispute with a neighbor, we can take it to a civil court and have our differences settled by a judge who is a hopefully impartial referee.

The problem with a civilian with a gun is that there is a possibility that they could become a prosecutor, a jury and a judge and an executioner, all with one squeeze of a trigger. Boom. It's over. A human is dead. We humans are emotional creatures. We can get upset, we can get offended, we can become confused about a situation. Many of us are old or have medical problems or failing eyesight or hearing problems and we are not always in a good position to resolve a dispute in a calm and impartial manner. Too often in recent history, an angry person with a machine gun has decided to execute crowds of people for no apparent reason, and it is hard for us to know in advance who these angry people might be or what might cause them to flip into mass assassins, and as a sad consequence, many innocent folks die for no reason whatsoever.

Freedom isn't about hiding out with a gun in a lone cabin, squinting through peepholes in wooden walls. Freedom comes from expanding our rights in the public sphere, stretching our bubbles of possible future action as far as we can without bumping into other peoples' bubbles, and agreeing to have an impartial referee of the legal system settle our disputes. We can do many more things when we work together in cooperative ways to accomplish mutually good goals.

Perhaps these ideas about voting and participating in politics and staying informed seem reasonable. Our society would be much better off if this is how most of us behaved.

But active citizenship requires commitment. Many of us might resent having to meet with fellow citizens for a half-hour every few months. It is a chore. We are humans. People tend to avoid work whenever they can. We can't merely participate only when we're passionate about a particular issue, and then slink back into nonparticipation when the passion fades.

A question, then, is how can we get ourselves up to the task of becoming real citizens? Our present arrangement is mostly voluntary as if citizenship means being free to personally define citizenship however we see fit.

With few exceptions, most of us do a rather shoddy job of being citizens, myself included. Only half of us bother to vote every four years for president, and even fewer of us vote every two years in the midterm elections. Many of us try to avoid jury duty. Some of us gravitate toward partisan propaganda organs instead of legitimate news sources, so we are not well-informed about current events. Even when we vote, we are often likely to choose a candidate based on past exposure to advertisements, or the ethnic sound of their last name, or some other irrelevant criteria such as how they look and talk on camera, rather than choosing candidates based on their policy positions.

The underlying issue here, which is well known, is the so-called Problem of the Commons. Essentially, when there's a public good, such as everybody participating in politics, but there's little direct reward for a particular person to do so, then there's a tendency for most persons to step back, to retreat into private life, and to focus on personal business rather than politics. We don't get paid to show up at a meeting of citizens but we do get paid to go to work. So we have a tendency to shirk our public duty and to let other people take our place in the political system.

Forces push us away from participation. Politics can get divisive, and people don't like conflict. Most of us don't like to get into arguments. It can get stressful. With our supposed freedom to be left alone, we can skip the meetings, go home, turn on our televisions to stream the latest movies, and reassure ourselves that we are still citizens because we have a government-issued passport.

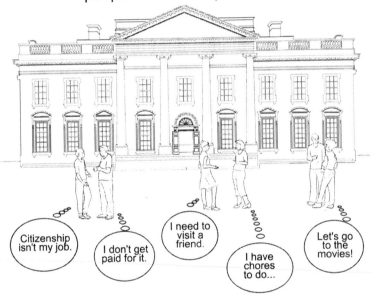

With no direct benefit for participating in politics, people retreat into private life

So how can we motivate ourselves to become real citizens? And continue to behave and act and think like real citizens?

With any construction project, of course, we break it up into smaller steps. The first step is to specify what citizenship means in the Constitution itself so there is clarity about what's involved.

Next, we offer a choice: Do people want to become citizens? Or would they prefer to be non-citizen residents? Being able to make a choice is critical, since some people might not be able to fulfill their citizenship duties, or they might not want to do what is required. Some might have religious qualms about fighting in a war; that's fine if that is their choice, but these people should not be able to vote for a war that they refuse to fight in. The idea is to align responsibility with political power.

Accordingly, there should be two distinct groups: citizens, and non-citizen residents. Non-citizen residents will most likely have to pay taxes, perhaps at a higher rate than that for citizens, and they can enjoy certain legal protections, but non-citizen residents should not be able to vote or hold office or serve on juries.

A benefit when we choose to be citizens is that we are more likely to value the relationship as well as know what is involved. Our hearts will be in it. At present, there is no act of choosing: What we have in the United States is, for most of us, called birthright citizenship, which means that all we have to do to become citizens is to be born here. That's it. There's not much choice about where we were born. We live to be eighteen years old and poof, we can vote. This understanding of citizenship is rather meaningless.

Citizenship is a bond between a person and the state. It is like other bonds, such as a marriage bond between two persons, or a bond of employment between a worker and a firm, or the bond of military service between a soldier and an army. In each of these cases there are signs indicating this relation: for example, married couples often wear wedding rings, and an employee might wear an identification badge, and a soldier might wear a uniform. Further, there are often ceremonies to mark the transition into the bond, such as a wedding, a get-acquainted meeting for a new employee, or an induction ceremony into the military. Citizenship should have similar markings as well as a public ceremony to emphasize its value and to bolster its importance in the public consciousness.

Accordingly, there should be a public ceremony to signify that a person is becoming a citizen. It should serve as a public reminder of the importance of the relationship. In the same way that a wedding informs people about this new relation between two human beings while emphasizing the value of love and the importance of family, a citizenship ceremony would alert people to this new relation and educate people about the privileges and responsibilities of citizenship.

A transition ceremony should require the inductee to swear an oath to affirm their personal commitment to uphold the values of democracy.

These include free and fair elections, voting, fairness and equal treatment, majority rule, individual rights, free speech, obeying the law, due process, a promise to fight in a war if summoned, and a pledge to uphold the Constitution. It should include a commitment to meet with fellow citizens to discuss politics on a regular basis and to serve on juries if summoned, as well as a promise to try to think in a rational manner using facts and logic with a respect for reality. The would-be citizen should promise to defend fellow citizens if the government becomes abusive.

Ideally a swearing-in citizenship ceremony should be officiated by a judge. There should be a government representative to affirm the government's part of the bargain: to protect the citizen; to settle disputes fairly; to obey the Constitution, which binds the government to treat citizens fairly; to support the citizen when they visit foreign lands; and to represent them in foreign courts if necessary. The public ceremony not only reminds the government of its duties, but it reeducates people about the nature of the citizenship relation.

The ceremony should reaffirm that citizenship is like a two-way contract between a free person and the state, with duties and privileges imposed on each in regard to the other party. It should be freely formed by both parties, freely maintained by both parties, and it can be dissolved by either party.

Fixing citizenship is a big task. Getting this right means that many of the other problems with American governance are likely to fix themselves. It is like fixing a huge underlying crack in the foundation of America, and repairing this crack means that many of the other superficial problems will be either easier to fix, or will fix themselves over time.

So the citizenship induction ceremony is over. Life returns to the day-to-day. Old habits return.

I promise to ....   The State promises to...

* Obey the law   * Obey the Constitution
* Fight in a war if summoned * Protect individual rights
* Vote   * Guard against foreign enemies
* Fulfill my jury duty   * Be an impartial referee in disputes
* Attend citizens' meetings * Represent citizens in foreign lands

How can we keep being citizens when many tasks are mundane and boring and tedious? Meeting with fellow citizens for a half-hour every few months can be regarded by some as a nuisance.

Accordingly, an aspect of these meetings should be an affirmation that we are indeed doing our duties: We're showing up, we're paying attention, we're keeping ourselves informed about current events, and we're thinking about public issues in a rational manner. We watch each other. And we can learn from each other by communicating. That's a benefit.

Much of my handyman knowledge I learned from plumbers and electricians and building inspectors and roofers and salespersons in hardware stores and other handypersons. A plumber taught me the one-thing-at-a-time rule. A client taught me to sprinkle salt when gluing two boards together so they don't slip when clamping. Some things I figured out through trial and error and I've shared these tips with others. For example, instead of washing out paintbrushes, I learned to load a brush with paint and then wrap it in a plastic bag, so it can be reused with the same paint for the next few weeks. I sometimes stick a used paintbrush inside a half-used paint can, which keeps it usable if the lid fits back on and if I don't tip the can when I store it—and if I mark the can with a note saying "paintbrush inside."

So at the citizens' meetings, we can learn from each other about the art of being good citizens and, in such a manner, become better citizens over time.

Further, there should be formal processes so that any citizen can challenge the citizenship status of another. If a delinquent citizen continues to shun meetings, fails to vote, does a haphazard job of keeping themselves informed, or disrupts the citizenship meetings, then another citizen should be able to challenge the citizenship status of the delinquent one, which could then lead to a judicial proceeding to determine what should be done. Stripping somebody of their citizenship should not be done lightly; there should be sufficient cause presented to justify such an action. But the underlying idea here is that one person shirking their citizenship duty while still having the status of a citizen, threatens all citizens by undermining the integrity of citizenship in general.

It should be the duty of citizens to keep other citizens in line. Most likely, the reprimanding of slacker citizens will occur only in a few cases, and few of those cases will survive through the judicial hurdles to actually cause a citizen to lose their citizenship through a legal proceeding. But the fear that this might happen might keep most of us in line, and spur us to keep doing our duty.

A more serious breach of citizenship might happen when a war breaks out, and citizens, who had pledged earlier to fight in a war, break their promise and refuse to fight. If this happens, then the state has an excellent case for punishing such persons. They had promised to fight. They didn't. They broke their promise. So the state can fine or imprison them with a clear legal justification.

Under the current system of birthright citizenship, however, we did not make any such pledge. We didn't do anything to become citizens. We were just born here. So in our own minds, as well as in the minds of everybody else, there is no commitment to fight in a war. Some might say, with war underway, that they don't want to fight in the war. If large groups of people decide that they don't want to fight, it could endanger the entire nation.

So the basic idea, as stated previously, is to link responsibility with political power. Defining citizenship, and emphasizing it in a proper swearing-in ceremony, brings clarity to the connection between a person and a state. If a person wants the power to vote and hold office and make political choices, then they must bear the responsibility of being a real citizen, and that means agreeing to fight in a war, if summoned.

Participating in political discussions is a skill that is best learned by doing it regularly. Though some aspects of debate can be learned in an educational setting such as a high school or college classroom, the crafting of rational arguments and the ability to persuade others of their merits is a skill that really needs to be practiced. Over time, we will get better at listening to arguments, dissecting them, crafting counterarguments, and learning the give-and-take of debate. There are highly educated people who think they are above this task of participating in democratic discussions. They've been to college. They may have advanced academic degrees. But they lack the skill of participating in a democratic forum.

Would greater citizen participation lead to better government? The answer is yes, almost certainly, since most people have common sense and an understanding of what is best for themselves and for others, and at the very least they are likely to make choices to benefit themselves. At present, few participate, which has led to rampant inequality to the point where many are ready to jettison the democratic system. Bringing disenfranchised Americans back into the political system would help even out the inequality in a political system that seems to value money over people. Widening participation, by itself, is not a guarantee of better government, since an important variable is whether new participants have civic virtue.

So a key task is to rebuild the system so that regular participation helps citizens become more virtuous. And that's what our fixes are designed to do: the more we participate, the more we learn how to be better citizens.

Now, let's get back to fixing our political house.

Major Repairs

WHEN I WAS REBUILDING THE porch, I found that the four brick columns were shaky and I had to replace them with concrete. I had to haul twenty heavy bags of concrete, but now I had a problem with bushes being damaged from the wheelbarrow. What I found is that trying to fix one thing often means having to fix other things too. If fixing the two-party system and citizenship and term limits are major parts of our porch fix, then other things will have to be fixed as well, so that the whole system works together coherently.

What we're talking about is a major renovation. But it is not a knock-down. There is no need to radically break apart and rebuild the entire structure. We need to keep the many good things with the current house. It is, after all, still standing, although it's shaky. The following things need to be kept.

The first good structure to keep is the idea of dividing the government into separate functions. The French political philosopher Montesquieu argued that one branch should make the laws, another enforce the laws, and a third interpret the laws. The Framers adopted this three-branch structure, which is why we have the legislature, the executive, and the judiciary. Each specializes in its particular area of governing. Power is split into multiple centers, reducing the risk of tyranny.

In much of human history, power was concentrated in one person. If a king or queen didn't like us, they could execute us with a wave of their hand. We wore the wrong clothes. We smiled at the wrong time. We befriended somebody they didn't like. So the king or queen made an instant decision that our past action had been illegal. Then they interpreted the law. They acted like the prosecutor, defense attorney, jury, and judge, all rolled into one nasty human, and then they enforced their retroactive "law" by summoning the executioner. It is easy to see why such power in one person is dangerous.

It is by the same reasoning that the Constitution rightly bans so-called retroactive laws, which happens when a ruling is made in the present that criminalizes people for their past behavior, and our renovation should keep this provision as well.

So what America has done, wisely, is to separate these powers into Congress, the presidency, and the Supreme Court. That's good. No single branch can bully us without oversight from the others. It prevents tyranny.

Another excellent thing America has done is to specify personal protections with the Bill of Rights. We can peaceably assemble. We can believe in whatever religion that we choose to believe in. We don't have to testify against ourselves in a court of law. We are protected from unlawful searches and 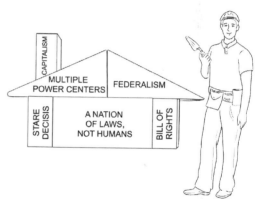 seizures of our property. And so on. These excellent rights can protect us from a sometimes overzealous majority. Though each of us belongs to different groups, which sometimes constitute a majority and sometimes a minority, each of us is a minority of one. The Bill of Rights should possibly be expanded with a citizen's right of privacy; at present this right is inferred from other rights but it would be better to specify this right, in writing, in a revised constitution.

There is a general idea throughout America that we are a nation of laws, not of humans, and that we make these laws collectively, and they apply equally to everybody, including to our government officials. So nobody is above the law. This is good.

An additional building block of our legal system that should be kept is a respect for past decisions, which legal scholars describe with the term *stare decisis*. When a new technology or situation arises and the written law is not clear, we can guess what the law will decide by examining past choices. This brings predictability and cohesiveness to the law in general, and it allows the legal code to evolve slowly in an understandable direction.

Another excellent part of the American system that should be kept is federalism. In this arrangement, the federal government is like a protective all-encompassing umbrella for the entire nation, while regulatory authority is pushed down to state governments. The beauty of this system is that it avoids a one-size-fits-all law for everybody and makes it possible for each state to decide what is best for their particular citizens. Each state can regulate with greater accuracy since each government is physically closer to its people. It is also safer for us since we can vote with our feet if our particular state's government regulates poorly or suboptimally; we won't have to keep enduring bad regulations since we can move to a state that regulates its economy better. Since states compete with each other to attract the best industries and workers and investors and people, this competitive pressure pushes states to enact sensible regulatory policies. Further, states have to spend wisely to keep from going bankrupt; there is no such pressure on the federal government, which has the power to print money when budgets get tight, so there is less risk of spending getting out of control.

Capitalism should be kept. It is a wonderful economic arrangement that has brought terrific prosperity and innovation to humankind. It rewards intelligent risk-taking and invention. It values resources. The nation has a long history of valuing free markets, entrepreneurship, business development, and individual initiative. These good things can be encouraged through the legal system with measures such as protections for patents and copyrights.

So in our renovation we should keep these excellent structures. Again, simply, we keep what works, and fix the flaws.

At this point let's briefly examine the Framers who crafted the original Constitution. It might help to know some of what they were thinking when they wrote the blueprints. They read top political thinkers such as Montesquieu and Locke. They studied the history of ancient Rome. They knew that they didn't want a king since they had felt directly and painfully, in their daily lives, the oppressive British system. They said things like "no taxation without representation." Many had direct experience with self-rule in their local and state governments.

But there are many things that the Framers didn't know. As I've said, they didn't know how the winner-take-all and first-past-the-post voting rules would force the nation into a two-party system. They distrusted organized factions that could corrupt the national interest, so their system, designed in large part by James Madison,

The Constitution's Framers were enlightened thinkers, but there were many things they didn't know.

worked to have factions compete against factions, and they were largely successful in this endeavor. The Framers gave Congress great power, but they distrusted it, so they put numerous shackles on its authority. They divided Congress into the two halves of the House and the Senate, and then gave the president the power to veto acts of the legislature.

There was a general understanding among the Framers that the Supreme Court could overturn acts of Congress by declaring their laws to be unconstitutional. But the power of judicial review was not clearly specified in the 1789 Constitution, and it was not discussed much in either the Constitutional Convention or during the ratification process. It was only later, in 1803, when Supreme Court Justice John Marshall described judicial review in its landmark decision of *Marbury v Madison*, that it became clearer what had been intended. Had this subject been understood better or debated further by those people who ratified the Constitution, then they may have decided against judicial review.

Judicial review is a check on the authority of the Congress. It means the Supreme Court can declare a law to be unconstitutional, thereby rendering the law invalid. Judicial review gives unelected judges awesome power to essentially do something that they're really not qualified to do, which is to make law, instead of merely interpreting the law. This check goes too far. It politicizes the judiciary. Few other established democracies in the world give their top judges such sweeping authority, and these democracies perform fine without judicial review. So in our renovation, let's remove judicial review.

The Framers were not perfect. Like all humans, they made mistakes. They didn't know everything. Many of them owned slaves. They counted enslaved African Americans as only three-fifths of a person, and they put this racist wording into the Constitution.

These points are important because Americans have a tendency to mythologize the Framers and see their creation, the Constitution, as some kind of sacred tablet, a perfect document, almost divinely inspired. It is easy to see why Americans tend to respect this document more than they should, since lawyers and lawmakers and the public often see the Constitution as being the highest law in the land, and they often settle their disputes by citing it.

But the Constitution is simply a set of laws undergirding a nation's laws. It is like the skeleton of a person or the concrete foundation of a building. It is not perfect. It is not something that we should adore with glazed eyes but examine in the cold hard light of truth.

When the original Constitution was written in 1787, the world was about to embark on huge changes that the Framers were not in a position to understand or prepare for. The Industrial Revolution was beginning. The nation would move away from farming, even though Thomas Jefferson thought that the country would remain a nation of independent farmers.

At the beginning, the nascent nation consisted of thirteen states on the eastern seaboard of North America, and it was separated from established European powers by the wide Atlantic ocean. So the Framers engineered the foreign policy function with the assumption that the nation would be protected by vast oceans. But today, with international travel, with intercontinental missiles that can attack in less than an hour, the oceans are not such an insurmountable barrier as they had been in the past. The world of today is considerably different from that of the Framers.

Further, the Constitution itself has evolved considerably. The franchise of who is eligible to vote has widened, from propertied white males, to all white males, to white and black males, and in the 20th century, to women. Despite these good changes, the level of civic participation has generally declined. It is only in times when people are substantially unhappy that they protest to try to fix things, and often these protests don't accomplish much. The few times when protests have resulted in positive change have happened when there was an aggrieved group that mounted a sustained effort for change, and even then progress can be slow. For example, it took women decades and decades to win the right to vote.

In the middle of the nineteenth century, the nation almost split apart because of the nagging issue of slavery. Arguably, if the Constitution had been designed better, without a two-party system, maybe the nation wouldn't have become as polarized regionally as it had become. It was lucky that back then the nation had savvy political leaders, particularly Abraham Lincoln, whose persistent policies kept the nation from cleaving in half. But it was a costly struggle in terms of lives lost and property damaged. One lasting effect of the five-year Civil War was that the idea of federalism was shaken, since many of the seceding southern states had done so under the banner of states' rights. And after the Civil War the federal government has increasingly assumed much greater authority over the states than the original Constitution had prescribed.

Another major flaw is the Senate skew. One could think of the original house of the United States as having had thirteen fairly well-balanced rooms. The thirteen original states had roughly the same populations, with four somewhat more populous states in Massachusetts and New York and Pennsylvania and Virginia, and the rest somewhat less populous states such as New Hampshire and Rhode Island.

But the Framers had to build in a compromise to appeal to the smaller states. They gave each state the same number of senators, two, regardless of the state's population or geographic size. So New York had the same representation in the Senate as Rhode Island. Though people in the less populous states had slightly more representation in the Senate, there was not much difference in Senate representation among the states, since the states were relatively equal in terms of population.

During the past twenty-four decades, however, there has been tremendous growth in population, and the distribution of people among the states has been highly uneven. Populous states like California have sixty-eight times more people than the sparsely settled state of Wyoming, even though both states have the same number of senators. The effect is that Wyoming voters have outsized clout in the Senate, and voters in populous states are relatively disenfranchised. It's as if the political system values land more than it values people.

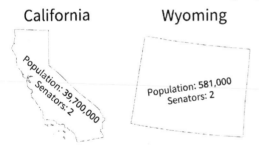

California

Wyoming

Population: 39,700,000
Senators: 2

Population: 581,000
Senators: 2

Voters in populous states like
California are seriously
underrepresented in the US Senate.

Since this imbalance gives an unfair advantage to the party that has more voters in rural states, this party is unlikely to approve of any effort to redress this imbalance. So nothing gets fixed.

If we think of the present-day United States as a fifty-room mansion, then some of the largest rooms like California and New York and Texas are spacious but don't get sufficient representation in the Senate. So badly needed resources that should have gone to these rooms get redistributed to smaller rooms where they bring much less value. The largest rooms suffer from relative neglect: the walls aren't well maintained, there is insufficient lighting, and floors creak as if to complain about a lack of funding, while the smaller rooms benefit from an overabundance of resources and projects. Money gets appropriated for rural highway projects while spending on bridges and tunnels in cities is neglected. It isn't fair for people in highly populated states to be underrepresented in Congress.

A further flaw is the nature of the primary system. Primary elections are preambles to the main election when voters from each party choose candidates for the main election. The Framers did not specify rules about presidential primaries, and in this void, a patchwork system emerged. A few states such as New Hampshire and Iowa hold their primaries so early in the election year, sometimes nine months before the general election, that they have achieved outsized influence in determining the presidency. An early win in Iowa or New Hampshire often gives a candidate an edge in the competition for campaign donations. As a result, candidates are forced to court voters in these rural states. Many voters in these states actually get to meet the candidates in person, shake their hands, listen to their speeches, and these candidates are likely to make promises to favor these states in terms of public policy after they get in office.

The failure to specify federal election rules means that the entire election process gets drawn out over a year, and even earlier, if one considers preparation time before the race begins. The result is that candidates face a grueling travel schedule of visits, fundraising, rallies, interviews with reporters, and other campaign-related tasks. The selection process favors neither the best possible politicians, nor the ones with the best ideas, nor those most likely to govern effectively, but the best campaigners.

In addition, since each state can choose when to hold their primaries, there is no sensible pattern. One week the primary is in New Hampshire, and the next week it could be in South Carolina, then Maine, then California. The extensive travel requires candidates to criss-cross the country repeatedly, which is time-consuming and expensive.

The Framers knew that circumstances would change, over time, and they specified mechanisms to change the Constitution to adapt to such circumstances. So they made it possible, yet difficult, for the nation to add amendments to the Constitution. This is good since it enables the nation to adapt to changing circumstances, and it is good that changes can not be made easily.

But did the Framers make amending the Constitution too difficult? Many Framers did not trust the public, so they insisted that three-fourths of the states had to agree to a change proposed by a two-thirds majority of each branch of Congress before an amendment could be ratified. But achieving such a majority is practically impossible with our highly polarized two-party system.

With the advantage of hindsight, we can see that there have been some good constitutional changes, such as the expansion of the voting franchise as noted earlier. There have been some dubious changes, such as the prohibition of alcohol in the 1920s that was reversed.

But the most revealing examples of the Constitution's inability to adapt itself positively over time are those in which pretty much everybody agrees that there is a problem but nothing changes. For example, problems noted previously, such as the haphazard primary system and the Senate skew, have been plainly evident for decades but they have not been fixed in the Constitution. Almost 700,000 people live in the District of Columbia, but they are denied representation in Congress because this area is not technically a state; this district has more Americans than the state of Wyoming. The problem with having only two parties is that one of them is likely to favor a change, while the other doesn't favor a change, and in this stalemate, nothing gets done. Each party has a veto power over constructive change, which results in gridlock and stalemate.

The glaring issue of gerrymandering has not been fixed despite strong consensus that it distorts elections. This flaw has been plainly evident for two hundred years, and yet our Constitution has not been amended to end or limit this form of legalized corruption. It is as if there's a major structural weakness in the house, causing a huge wall to sag, and everybody sees the sagging, but we collectively shrug our shoulders and don't fix it. With only two political parties, once politicians are elected, they have little incentive to fix gerrymandering. Maybe that's how they got elected. Maybe that's how they'll stay elected. So they are reluctant to change things even though they know it's unfair. So what? It keeps them in power.

The general problem is that incumbent politicians don't like competitive elections. They're in power. They want to stay in power. It is tempting and easy for them to engineer the rules to make their reelections easier. They don't want a level playing field. They want to win. So they use their power to make their reelections more likely. Who loses? We do. We have fewer choices.

So an important fixture in any constitutional revamp is term limits. The more powerful the office, the more it should be checked by term limits, although there should be a few exceptions to this rule, since some branches of government will need continuity, which will be addressed later.

Further, any constitutional revamp should be such that the Constitution can fix itself over time. This is going to be difficult since we, at this time in history, have limited foresight. We can't foresee what problems might occur, so how do we design a system that adapts itself successfully to changes that we can not imagine now? One way is to insist upon a substantive rethinking, perhaps every hundred years, with a new constitutional convention, so that the nation has regular opportunities to analyze the system in its entirety, and to make effective changes.

If we look back at our 240-year-old house, we see that it has grown considerably. It still stands. There have been small fixes, adding a closet here, replacing a wall there, adding a plumbing system, and so forth. Each fix had its own logic but these changes, taken together, have not always been what was best for the system as a whole.  An additional closet might have made another bedroom too small to use. A replaced wall might have stressed the foundation. The new plumbing system might have been useful but holes in the walls might let in cold air and termites. The external environment was changing too. The neighborhood has become crowded.

If any one government office has too much power, it is dangerous. The office of the presidency is too powerful.

It is as if one room in the house of the government has grown too large, squeezing out adjoining rooms. This was not always the case. During the nineteenth century, the presidency was one of three co-equal branches of government, sharing power with Congress and the judiciary. But since the 1930s and into the twenty-first century, the presidency has assumed unparalleled power.

The American president has…

- Vast authority over a slew of federal agencies, including the Justice Department
- The power to appoint judges to the Supreme Court
- The power to appoint leaders of various federal agencies
- Veto power over Congressional legislation unless both chambers can muster two-thirds of their members to override the veto
- The power to either recommend or shun primary congressional challengers from their own party, which gives the president considerable control over which party members get elected to Congress
- The ability to issue pardons
- Vast spending authority
- Command of the armed forces
- The largest share of power over foreign policy, including the ability to start foreign wars
- The bully pulpit, enabling the president to focus national attention on any issue
- The ability to issue executive orders
- Signing statement power, so that when they sign a bill, they state how they intend to enforce it, effectively undermining the will of Congress

It should be that an office with such power would require that people who assume this office be qualified for the position, and have good character and competence as a leader. But there are surprisingly few requirements for someone to become the president. They don't have to have a working knowledge of the law, or have previous experience in government, or have the approval of their own party's leaders, or be skilled in statecraft or knowledgeable about the military arts, or have a working familiarity with world affairs. There is no vetting process.

So pretty much anybody can run for president, provided they were born in the United States and are at least 35 years old. There is no formal process where unsuitable candidates get screened out other than the voters. Being president is a tough and demanding job that requires much experience and political skill and an ability to work with a va-

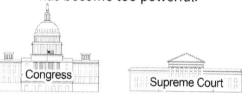

The office of the American president has become too powerful.

riety of people, and few people have the mental acumen and internal discipline to handle it.

So the only real requirement for the office of the presidency is winning the election. Their chief skill is winning over voters with speeches and advertising and promises and appeals. That's what they're good at. They're not necessarily good at governing, at being the head of the military, or managing foreign policy.

In the past, there have been a few excellent presidents, many mediocre, and some positively bad presidents.

Further, presidents have three extremely huge responsibilities. They are the ...

- Head of a political party
- Head of the domestic government
- Head of foreign policy

Each task is difficult enough on its own, and having one person manage these three demanding tasks is nearly impossible. Each task requires a different mindset. Being the head of a political party, one must be a devout partisan to advocate for that party's agenda, and this requires a salesperson's mentality and marketing skills. Being the head of the domestic government requires knowledge of how the government works, how to compromise, how to form coalitions, and how to understand sometimes intricate and detailed policy proposals and the mechanics of passing legislation. Being the head of foreign policy requires a knowledge of history, military developments, strategy, treaties and tariffs, and statecraft.

These mindsets are different, often opposing, and it is difficult to find one official who can handle all three tasks simultaneously.

Further, some of these responsibilities conflict with others. Foreign policy should be what's best for the whole nation, not just a part, but the president's task of being the head of a political party can be a conflict. A political party, a part-y, is about what's best for a particular part of the nation, not about what's best for the nation as a whole. There have been instances in the past where a president's partisanship led to foreign policy blunders—for example, the administration of President George W. Bush outed one of our own espionage agents, Valerie Plame, because she was married to an official of the opposite party.

So it is little wonder why America's foreign policy has been flaky, haphazard, varying from mediocre to sometimes good, over the past hundred years. There is a certain randomness to it, a lack of a consistent and coherent pattern that would keep it fixed to a steady focus. Foreign policy blunders are evident. America has a tendency to get involved in seemingly endless and expensive foreign wars such as in Korea and Vietnam and Iraq and Afghanistan, most often with inconclusive results. We have a knack for supporting dictators around the world, since they're often easier to work with than leaders of other democracies. Ideally statecraft should consistently reward friends while deterring enemies, but the United States has trouble with that.

Foreign policy is not an abstract subject that doesn't affect us. It does. When the country gets embroiled in endless wars, Americans like us die. It costs money, and the funds wasted could have been used to build infrastructure such as highways and bridges and schools and high-speed rail, or used to advance medicine or improve the Internet. Instead it gets wasted on things that blow up and kill people.

Further, the nation cannot keep long-term commitments to allies because of its constitutional structure. Every four years, there's a chance that there will be a new president, and with that, a new foreign policy. Since there is a two-term limit for the presidency, then every eight years there must be a new president, again with a likely shift in the government's foreign policy. So it is hard to keep long-term commitments to allies and to stick to plans that take decades to bring to fruition. It is as if the nation has an ADHD-rattled brain that can't keep a coherent and steady focus on the distant future. The result is a scattershot foreign policy that is hit or miss, that sometimes makes wise choices, sometimes not.

So American statecraft, when successful, is often a matter of luck. The public chooses the president not based on their foreign policy skill but rather on their skill as a campaigner. So, by happenstance, sometimes the elected presidents are knowledgeable about foreign affairs, but sometimes they are not. Even when we have a president who is competent at statecraft, their focus is often distracted since they have to deal with domestic matters as well as party politics. It is usually the case that the leaders we have entrusted with national security are learning on the job.

We should not blame the Framers for crafting this flawed foreign policy structure. Back when they wrote the Constitution, it wasn't flawed since the young nation was protected by vast oceans, and it had no serious military threats in North America. Their concerns were dividing power to prevent tyranny, and the Constitution did a good job of doing that. The Framers lived when travel between the states took weeks, so they allowed plenty of time between the presidential election and the inauguration, approximately ten weeks; today, however, this awkward interval features essentially two presidents, a lame duck president soon to be out of office, and an incoming president, and it is not always clear who is in charge. Times have changed.

So it's pretty clear that the architecture of foreign policy must be overhauled substantially. This will require rebuilding part of the foundation. It is a huge change. And such a large change will mean that we probably have to adjust other structures in the government as well.

So we've pulled up most of the floorboards and we have a fairly good look at the numerous flaws with our current political structure: the too-powerful presidency with often conflicting responsibilities, incumbent politicians rigging the system to keep themselves in office, unelected justices overturning laws of the legislature, rural voters having outsized representation in the Senate, a haphazard primary system, no foreign policy qualifications for the president, clueless out-to-lunch citizens, the federal government intruding into the regulatory authority of the state governments to impose often clumsy one-size-fits-all rules, an ADHD-like shortsighted foreign policy that leads to blunders and extended inconclusive foreign wars and dubious alliances with dictators, no term limits, and the flawed two-party system of representation that forces voters to choose between two mainstream parties.

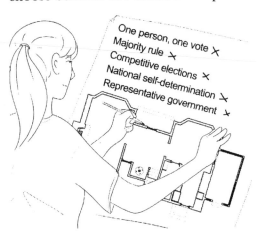

This current system violates many of the basic principles of a good government: one person, one vote; majority rule; competitive elections; national self-determination; and representative government. It is why people feel powerless. The system fosters a political class of professional politicians whose first focus is not what is best for us, but what will help them keep being reelected. We the people are pushed out of the system. Money takes our place. So well-heeled donors have much influence in what decisions get made.

Crafting the Blueprints

OUR PROJECT IS NOT A knockdown. We're not going to bulldoze our house and rebuild it from scratch. Rather, it's a renovation. But it's not tinkering with a wall here or a door there. We're talking about a *major* renovation. Anything less won't fix the problems. We'll need to revise the blueprints—that is, the Constitution.

But what do we do first? There are many ways to do this. Different architects will have different ideas and many of them could work. Though we might hope that serious constitutional scholars and political scientists will craft a good plan, many of them have become so specialized in their academic fields that they get lost in the details. Seeing the big picture is hard, and it helps to have worked on a variety of old houses.

The way we might approach our renovation is to focus first on the vital structures, and then adapt the existing structures to the new one. The idea is to keep the best of the existing house while building in a sensible addition, so that the entire structure works together in harmony, while ensuring that it is a safe place for us to live in.

Our nation should be strong. A solid foreign policy architecture is like reinforced concrete. So when foreign nations press against it, it stays firm, because concrete has excellent compressive strength. But it also needs to be strong from within, to keep internal forces from pulling it apart, so it needs steel rebar with its excellent tensile strength to hold it together. That's the domestic government. We need both together. We need excellent foreign policy and excellent domestic policy, with both parts working together.

Let's start with the foreign policy architecture since this is the branch of government that, in my view, has the most problems. It is vital that the nation gets foreign policy right. As Americans, we are so used to seemingly endless wars fought away from our shores that perhaps we have lost the clear-eyed sense that bad foreign policy could bring death and destruction to our homeland. History books bulge with stories of seemingly invincible kingdoms and nations that were swiftly and unexpectedly reduced to ruin.

At present, statecraft is made by an often inexperienced partisan president, and that authority is dispersed among different branches of government, since the Senate can ratify treaties and the Supreme Court can rule on international disputes.

Statecraft is difficult. Throughout history, few nations or empires have been good at it. Perhaps the best one was the Roman Republic, which lasted close to five hundred years until it degenerated into an empire.

A proposed State Department

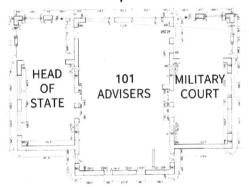

HEAD OF STATE · 101 ADVISERS · MILITARY COURT

So the first step is to consolidate the statecraft apparatus into a single branch of government. At present, there is a State Department but it does not have exclusive authority over foreign policy. It serves under the president, and when the presidency changes hands, so do its top officials. What we want is for statecraft to be managed by nonpartisan officials who are experienced and smart and good, who stay in office for decades so they know what they're doing. We don't want its officials learning on the job.

The State Department should have the exclusive task of managing foreign policy. That should be its only job. That should be what it does, and does competently. No other branch should have this function or be able to interfere with its decision-making. That way, it can be held accountable by the rest of the government for its performance. If things go wrong, it can't blame another official or branch, or diffuse blame throughout the government.

This branch should have authority over every aspect of foreign policy: international affairs, ambassadors and the foreign service, diplomacy, trade and tariffs, military policy, espionage, immigration, and strategic planning. It makes these policies and enforces them. It manages the officials who manage these tasks, such as consuls and spies and quartermasters and generals and border guards.

For this branch to be effective, it needs to juggle two possibly conflicting aspects: having long-term smarts as well as the ability to act quickly in an emergency or a war. So we divide it into two separate functions:

- **A council of foreign policy advisers.** They're experts who understand world politics. They understand military developments, strategic threats and opportunities, and the past history of international affairs. Accordingly, these advisers need to stay in these positions for long periods of time to get the expertise to be effective. The council would benefit by having disparate viewpoints, so their number should be large enough to represent different views, perhaps one hundred and one advisers, with the odd number to prevent a tie if the group votes on a decision. They should be appointed when they are relatively young, perhaps in their thirties or forties, and hopefully they'll remain in these positions for several decades. They should be highly paid so that they are hard to bribe, while their overall wealth should be capped at a reasonable level to prevent abuse. As older members retire or die or become unable to do their jobs, they can be replaced by younger members, and in that way, the group as a whole preserves its institutional memory. It would be like a wise man who never dies, to use de Tocqueville's phrase, since the older members can educate the younger members about the world situation.

- **A head of state.** This official will be in charge of overall policy. They will be a commander in wartime, directing the nation's war effort, coordinating campaigns. The advantage of having a single official in charge is to expedite action in an emergency. In peacetime, the head of state represents the nation to other nations, meets with foreign officials, and is the face of the foreign policy branch of the government.

The foreign policy advisers should be in charge of selecting the head of state. They won't be able to choose one of their own members, or a president or a senator or a representative, because such a choice would lead to a conflict of interest. Rather the advisers would choose a qualified outsider to lessen the chance of internal power struggles within their own ranks.

The advisers bring continuity. The head of state brings fast action. Together they enable the nation to have a smart long-term strategic focus. They can carry out plans that take decades to implement. They can be patient. They can react to fast-moving circumstances. The nation won't have an ADHD-like flaky impermanence to policy-making. Rather, they can make a policy and stick with it for decades, so an ally can count on its promises and an enemy can fear its long-term wrath. Most likely the State Department will feel no need to coddle foreign dictators. Foreign policy will likely be coherent and focused. The nation could consistently advocate for the cause of human rights and really mean it.

Such a structure does not guarantee excellent foreign policy but it is likely to improve overall foreign policy. It is a sensible structure. The officials who run foreign policy are more likely to protect the nation and avoid needless wars. They could cope with pressing international issues such as climate change and terrorism, and be less subject to partisan pressures. The State Department will have its own court that will decide cases involving foreign affairs, such as when foreigners visit us or when we visit foreign nations, or immigration matters, or cases involving spies and espionage, or interpretations of treaties, and so forth.

The new system will work like this: citizens elect domestic government officials who, in turn, choose foreign policy officials. We are not giving up our power to choose our foreign policy leaders but rather we are going to elect them only indirectly.

There are reasons why this indirect arrangement is highly preferable.

Let's be honest with ourselves. Foreign policy is not something we're good at. We don't know. Most Americans have a lackluster understanding of even basic geographic information. Foreign policy is too complex of a subject for most citizens, including enlightened ones who try to stay informed, so it does not make sense for policy choices to be made by public debate and subsequent voting. We do not have enough information and patience to select who is best to lead our foreign policy.

If our nation is like a single human, then we as citizens are like the cells of that human's body. We know whether we're happy or not, whether we're getting enough food and water and air. But we don't really know how the body should deal with life. As individual cells, we are not able to make decisions for the body as a whole. Rather, such decisions are the proper tasks of the brain, and in this analogy, the brain is the national government.

Let me examine my own understanding. I have a fairly in-depth knowledge of history, and a solid grounding in the basics of science, but my sense of current affairs worldwide is mostly vague and spotty. I have a general sense that I don't like dictators and that I support the cause of freedom and human rights, but I don't know the particulars of specific world leaders, or what issues are facing foreign countries, or how to handle a problematic region like the Middle East. I have neither studied the area in depth nor have had the time for such study or an inclination to do so. If there was a public discussion about how to handle the Middle East, you would not want my opinion influencing debate, and I would probably not like your opinion doing similarly. Me, you, we, all of us: we just don't know. So we should not influence foreign policy by choosing its officials by voting.

It is of little surprise then that the historical record of democracies that have tried to make sensible foreign policy is lackluster. A case in point: the city-state of ancient Athens was fighting a tough war with Sparta, and in the middle of the war, its citizens voted to launch a naval expedition against an ally of Sparta, the city-state of Syracuse. This city was roughly the same size as Athens. Athenians made a foolish choice. Their foolhardy expedition against Syracuse resulted in a catastrophic defeat.

In a democracy, majority rule is vital for making domestic policy. We the people can make sensible choices on matters like how to regulate businesses or build highways or whether dogs should run free in public parks. This is our territory. We have a sense of what to do because we feel the consequences up close and personally, each day. But we don't know about international affairs. Even if we did know, we often could not make decisions quickly enough because debate and discussion, followed by voting, takes too long. What we need is a sharp group to keep us out of war, and if war happens, to have a savvy commander who makes decisions correctly and quickly. That's the State Department.

We've fixed a major fault in the foundation of our house. But making the foreign policy apparatus strong will stress the other branches. The risk is that this branch will become so powerful that it might grow to dominate the government, or cause corruption or tyranny. It's like we've added a wing to our mansion that risks overpowering the existing structure, so we have to upgrade that as well.

If we empower the State Department, we have to check that power. For that purpose, we check the officials within it but not their decision-making. We don't want domestic officials making foreign policy, but we want them to be able to hold foreign policy officials accountable if those officials are doing a bad job. A risk is that State Department officials might abuse their authority to enrich themselves or overpower the rest of the government, so we must build in strong safeguards to keep this from happening or to cope with it if it does.

Let's assume that our revamped Constitution requires active citizenship, as defined previously. Suppose we're real citizens now. We pay attention to politics, we read newspapers and digital media sources, and we've promised to protect each other in case the government becomes abusive. We are learning the art of having reasoned discussions on political subjects without it degenerating into a cacophony of personal attacks.

So now the task is to strengthen the domestic government so that it is strong enough to represent us, and skilled enough to oversee the newly powerful State Department. We can't have a domestic government that is itself helplessly divided, unable to make decisions, hamstrung, with different parts at loggerheads in unconstructive ways. It should have a cohesiveness of purpose, and not be hampered by gridlock and stuck in perpetual stalemate. It's got to have its act together. And yet it needs to reflect a diversity of views if it is to act as a good mirror of the public. It needs to be our government, working for us. So we need to describe how the various parts of the government interrelate to each other and how we as citizens relate to these parts.

Let's focus on how we interact with our government as citizens. While there are a variety of ways to structure our political life to strengthen domestic government, the proposed arrangement will be effective and sturdy and workable, with minimal time constraints on us as citizens, that fixes the many problems with our current system.

As stated earlier, democratic systems can be weakened by forces that push people away from participation. Debate can be frustrating and tedious, disagreements can happen, boredom can set in. People would rather stay home or work at their jobs or go on vacation.

So we must build in enticements to encourage participation. It won't work if people walk away from the process disgruntled, shaking their heads in frustration. A motivation is that it's for our personal betterment to have political clout. We could make friends at these meetings. If we don't participate, we risk losing our citizenship. Accordingly, we attend a half-hour meeting every four months.

The next change is from a two-party system to a multiparty system. We achieve this by abandoning the winner-take-all election system and choosing proportional representation. That way, the legislature will more closely mirror the public. With more choices, it is more likely that we'll find a party that better represents us. Voting for a third or a fourth or a fifth party won't be wasting our vote. It's a better mirror—not perfect, but better.

Before:
Two-party system

Democratic Party

OR

Republican Party

After:
Multiparty system

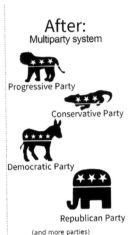

Progressive Party

Conservative Party

Democratic Party

Republican Party
(and more parties)

In a multiparty system, some parties will be larger with many members while others will be smaller. The bigger ones will have more influence in the domestic government, but at least the smaller parties will have a say in what happens, and their opinions may get a fair hearing. It could happen that the views of the large parties are wrong or short-sighted or problematic, and the advantage of having legislators from smaller parties is that the faulty views of the major parties could be challenged, and possibly fixed. Conversely, if the views of the major parties are beneficial, then challenges from the smaller parties will help to strengthen and clarify these correct views.

Nevertheless, a political party can't be too small. Though it is conceivable to have a party of only one person, it would be unworkable politically for obvious reasons. It doesn't make sense to have hundreds and hundreds of tiny parties. How could they all be listed on a ballot? Voters would waste time trying to read through the choices. There should be a minimum size requirement in terms of members for a party to be recognized as official.

So we specify a minimum size for a political party—let's say two percent of the overall voting public. With this requirement, there could be a maximum of fifty different parties, each meeting the two percent threshold exactly. But in practice, most likely there will be a few larger parties and maybe a half-dozen smaller ones. That would give voters more choices while being manageable. The two percent requirement might need to be raised to three percent if it causes too many tiny parties, or lowered to one percent if it results in too few parties.

Accordingly, if two percent or more of citizens belong to a specific party, then that party becomes an official party for at least the next two years, and it can nominate candidates for Congress. Since the congressional election cycle is two years, then a fledgling party will have a chance to get a candidate or candidates on the ballot in that time interval.

Next, let's focus on Congress. At present, there are 435 representatives in the House and 100 senators in the Senate. Let's keep it that way. There's no need to change things just for changing things. That's in keeping with our handyperson fix-up rule: keep what works, fix the flaws.

Further, in the House of Representatives, let's keep apportionment by state population. That's the current system. More populous states get more representatives, and less populous states get fewer representatives. Each state gets at least one.

Every ten years the nationwide census determines how many citizens live in each state. At present, the census counts how many *people* live in each state, but the census will be revised in the new system to count not just people but *citizens*. States will probably have the same number of representatives with the new system as with the old system, because the proportion of citizens to people will probably be the same nationwide, assuming, of course, that most people will choose to become citizens. States will probably encourage their residents to become national citizens, since it will give their states greater clout in the House.

With House representation based on population, as determined by the census every ten years, highly populous states like California and Texas and New York and Florida will get many representatives, while less populous rural states like Wyoming will get fewer representatives, and every state will have at least one representative, as it is at present. When decisions are made, the majority will still rule, since that is our collective best guess of what's best for all of us. Though those guesses may be wrong or short-sighted, they're still our best guesses. What the majority chooses is probably something that most of us want, so at a minimum, those choices are likely to please at least half of us.

Of course there are several hundred million of us, and only 435 representatives. Each of us, as an individual political actor, has hardly any clout, so we express ourselves politically through political parties. We join the one that wants what we want, which we think will advocate for our positions. With enough citizens in a party, it will have clout. The respective sizes of these various political parties should be reflected in the legislature with party proportional representation. So if 28% of citizens belong to the Lower Utility Bills party, then approximately 28% of the House representatives will belong to that party.

To achieve party proportional representation, we abandon geographically defined congressional districts. If we cordon off an area within a state, and ask voters to choose a single representative by majority rule to represent that geographic area, then this results in the winner-take-all arrangement. That one person in that one district will represent only those voters that chose him or her. We can not divvy up that representative's mind to advocate for those who didn't choose him or her.

By removing the gerrymandered congressional district boundaries, we can achieve party proportional representation within states like New Jersey.

There are other reasons for abandoning geographically defined congressional districts. Drawing these districts on a map is problematic, since it encourages incumbent politicians to finagle with boundary lines to help their political allies or frustrate their opponents. Though nonpartisan redistricting is a step in the right direction, the spectre of gerrymandering remains, since determining the partisanship status of an official is based on guesswork. Ranked choice voting is a possible improvement, but there are problems there too, since the math behind the process can be difficult to understand and hard to explain, and it could lead to partisan fussing about whether the procedures are fair. It is possible to use mathematics and computer modeling to define boundaries, to minimize travel time within the district while making each district equally sized in terms of population, but even such a plan could be problematic: for example, if some regions are mountainous or separated by wide rivers, how would the program handle exceptions like that? An algorithm could draw a supposedly fair electoral district that would bunch together people on different sides of a mountain, which would be inconvenient. For many reasons, we really don't need these artificial boundaries when it comes to voting, but the overriding reason is that these geographic districts prevent party proportional representation.

Accordingly, to prevent gerrymandering, and to enable party proportional representation, we remove congressional district boundaries. Now each state's representatives will represent all citizens within their state. For example, I live in New Jersey, and according to the 2020 census, my state gets twelve representatives. So all twelve are my representatives. I can go to any of them for questions or assistance with any matter. But these twelve are not exclusive to me, of course, since they represent all of New Jersey. Like me, my neighbor can go to any of the twelve with an issue.

With such an arrangement, with the congressional boundary lines gone, it's possible to have party proportional representation within each state. We match party representatives to voters within New Jersey to get a fairly accurate mirroring.

This is how it could work. When New Jerseyans go to the polls, each voter would vote for one party. Votes would be tallied. If Party X got 50%

of the votes, it would get 50% of the state's twelve representatives, or six representatives. If Party Y got 25% of the votes, it would get three representatives. If Party Z got 10% then it might get one representative, and so forth. State lawmakers would set rules for how to handle rounding issues. It is an approximation, of course, since no mirroring is exact, but it is a much better mirror than what we have now.

The proportion of party representatives to voters' preferences will match more closely in highly populous states like California and Texas and New York. In California, which has 53 representatives, the mirroring will be much more exact. In less populous states, the match will be less exact. In states like Wyoming, which has only one representative, it will be as if the winner-take-all rule applies. The entire state of Wyoming is a single congressional district, and whatever party wins the most votes, wins the entire state. But for the nation as a whole, it is likely that there will be excellent proportionality, with legislators mirroring the electorate.

A benefit of a multiparty system based on party proportional representation is that the House of Representatives will be more likely to think like we think. This is getting back to representative democracy. It is good.

An important change is voting for a party rather than a person. There are reasons why this is better. Since the Framers distrusted political parties, they sought to limit their influence. But political parties are not inherently bad; they are merely a group of like-minded voters, and a party is a vehicle for them to push a particular program through the government. Though a particular party's agenda might be harmful, such as a party that tries to swing a wrecking ball at the democratic system itself to establish a dictatorship, the existence of a party, in itself, is not a bad thing.

The basic reason to emphasize parties rather than people is that it encourages voters to think about issues instead of personalities. When voters see a candidate's name on the ballot, they may vote based on the candidate's name, their gender, their speaking style, their racial or ethnic affiliation, or for some other irrelevant reason. If they have seen a photo of the candidate, they may choose based on physical attractiveness, or how they appeared in a television commercial.

Such characteristics are distractions. They shift the focus away from issues. The best way for voters to express their political preferences is to vote for a party that expresses those preferences. Of course a voter could still vote for a party because they like its candidates' charm or clothing style or hairdo or ethnic background, but the subtle benefit over time is to encourage voters to think in terms of issues, and to vote accordingly.

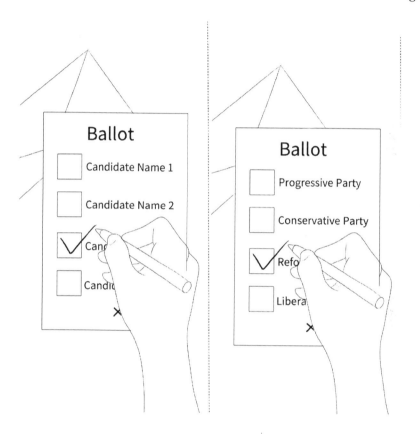

We can amplify the focus on issues rather than personalities by requiring voters to identify with a particular political party. This again turns the focus on issues rather than personalities by encouraging us to think about what we want, and to express what we want by declaring a party affiliation. So instead of everybody thinking in terms of white voters, or women voters, or senior citizen voters, or rural voters, or voters of

Italian descent, or religious voters, we'll have voters who favor less pollution, or voters who favor spending on transportation, or voters who favor the legalization of marijuana. The huge benefit is that it encourages all of us to stop thinking in terms of things we can't change or have great difficulty changing, such as our sex or race or ethnic background or sexual orientation or religious views, and it encourages us to start thinking about issues that we can change, such as how the country should deal with energy or climate change or pollution or fiscal spending on airports. We can't change a person's ethnic background but we can change their thinking about healthcare policy.

Accordingly, every citizen, including candidates running for office, will declare membership in a specific political party. This will be public information accessible by everybody. This declaration will be made at every meeting of citizens, and it should be published, perhaps using computerized digital technology, so up-to-date counts can be reported in the media.

A benefit of such regular declarations is that political parties can be recognized quickly. The nation will have a fairly accurate and current assessment of what the public thinks. If any party gets two percent of all declarations nationwide at any particular time, then it becomes an official party, which means that it can advance candidates for election and have slots on the ballot. At the next election, its candidates can be elected to public office at the state or national level. It becomes a viable party.

These regular declarations are valuable information for the entire political process. It makes it easy for journalists and politicians and judges and institutions and citizens in general to have a quick grasp of what the public wants. It's as if the public has a mirror showing us what we are currently thinking. If an issue becomes prominent and citizens declare membership in a party that addresses that issue, then a new political party can suddenly bloom into life. If its candidates are elected to public office, then it might have a chance to do something about this issue. This will increase the overall responsiveness of the political system, since we won't have to wait for years and years for problems to be identified and fixed.

That new parties can spring up out of nowhere will keep existing political parties on their toes. They will have to stay in touch with what people want. If a political party declines in popularity to the point where its share of membership declarations falls below two percent, and if this percentage stays below two percent for a twenty-four month period, then that party is removed from the public roster and it loses its status as an official party.

This competition among political parties to attract and keep members is highly beneficial for all of us. These parties will keep courting us, trying to win us over, trying to persuade us to choose them. That's healthy politically. It empowers us as citizens. In the current system, the two mainstream parties can substantially ignore our needs because their candidates will get reelected regardless of what most of us want.

There's one other thing. In our present political world, many folks opt out of the system. Some of us don't vote. Some don't pay attention to public issues. Some don't stay informed. And one way of ditching our duty of participating politically is to declare ourselves as independent, which means that we don't identify with any particular party.

But in the new system, we can't let this happen for extended periods of time. Citizens who continue to refuse to declare an allegiance to a specific political party, or who declare themselves as unaligned or noncommittal or independent, are essentially passively refusing to participate in public life. They're on the sidelines. They're not playing the political game.

As citizens, we must choose a specific political party. There must be no ducking this requirement. This is important since it lets everybody know where we stand on the issues. We know what a particular citizen is about. It says, in effect, that a citizen thinks X, and this gives proponents of X a measure of confidence that their positions are supported, and it gives opponents of X a chance to persuade the citizen otherwise. And it helps us clarify to ourselves what we think.

Further, we must choose an official political party at least half of the time at these meetings. The purpose is to prevent a citizen from passively opting out of the political process by consistently choosing an obscure party with no chance of electoral success. Since such a party is unlikely to reach the two percent threshold, it won't win elections. But letting citizens choose an unofficial party half of the time lets small parties gain recognition and possibly become an official party later on. Declarations for unofficial parties might nudge official parties to modify their positions to win over such voters. But a citizen who consistently declares membership in non-official parties, year after year, is really shirking their responsibility as a citizen, and it should be possible for others to challenge that person's citizenship on that basis.

Accordingly, citizens are free to declare allegiance to any political party of their choosing, half of the time, which allows nascent parties a chance to grow while preventing citizens from passively opting out of participation. So during a two-year interval, they could choose an unofficial party for three of their meetings but they must choose an official party at the remaining three meetings, or they could alternate between an official and an unofficial party for each meeting. Since all citizens must vote every two years, their only choices will be from the list of officially recognized parties, so there is a built-in incentive by the voting process itself to encourage people to choose an official party.

Let's make a few choices to make voting simpler and clearer. For example, names of political parties shall not exceed thirty characters in length. Such a requirement may appear to be trivial, but the benefit is to simplify the task of declaring loyalty to a party and to lessen the risk of errors caused by misspellings. We don't want party names to become like long trains of words that we have to remember, and yet thirty characters is sufficient alphabetic real estate to enable millions of possible combinations. It lessens the chance that parties will turn their names into mini-advertisements.

Further, each political party should have a position statement explaining briefly what they hope to achieve in the public sphere. Again, we don't want such statements to go on page after page since we're busy. So let's pick a maximum length of five hundred characters, which is like a few sentences or a short paragraph. That's plenty of space for the party to describe itself while minimizing reading. When we're doing politics, we don't want to read a novel. Of course, the party could write other statements going into greater depth about its positions or strategies or agendas, which we might read, if we wish, but we don't have to. The idea here, of course, is to make our task of being citizens as easy as possible.

Before we proceed, let's take stock of where we stand. Dear reader, would you be willing to act like a real citizen? Would you be willing to attend half-hour meetings every four months? Would you be willing to declare membership in an official political party at least half the time?

My sense is that most of us are used to opting out of the political process. This has been my pattern. For years, I didn't pay much attention to politics. When I voted, I sometimes chose a write-in candidate to express my dismay with the two-party system, knowing full well that the write-in candidate had no chance of winning. I was a slacker citizen. Most likely, so were you.

But when most people behave like us, problems fester, and all manner of weirdness slips into the public sphere. And yet the political process goes on nevertheless. Players with specific agendas can insert themselves between the people and the politicians. By hiring lobbyists, corporations can get their taxes lowered or prevent competitors from challenging them in their markets. Foreign dictators can foster discontent and resentment. We see what happens: rampant inequality, frivolous and wasteful wars, us-versus-them political polarization, poorly educated citizens, periodic episodes of gun violence, underperforming schools, shoddy healthcare, decaying highways and bridges, substandard trains, crowded and expensive prisons, and the list goes on and on.

So you should hold me accountable to be a real citizen, and I should do likewise for you. We all need to do this for each other. This is the only way to revive the public sphere and to begin to make our political world work for us, and not for corporate lobbyists or foreign dictators or weapons manufacturers or professional politicians or billionaires.

We all need to be handypersons on the jobsite of America. So let's focus on elections. At present there is a two-year interval for congressional elections. This is a reasonable amount of time for a representative to effect change in the legislature. The interval is short enough so that the legislature can be refreshed every two years to reflect the changing will of the public.

Elections happen in the first week of November of every second year. So let's keep it that way. But the choice of Tuesday is not optimal since many people have to work during the week, so citizens should be able to vote at any time during that first week of November.

Should voting be public or private? There are tradeoffs. If each citizen makes a public declaration about their choice, then everybody can know who they voted for, so the process is transparent. This is good because there is little chance of behind-the-scenes fraud or manipulation of vote recording machinery. In a sense, it is a stronger vote than a private-secret vote because it suggests that the voter is not afraid to publicly affirm their choice. There is no doubt about its legitimacy. Everybody knows where everybody stands.

But a benefit of secret voting is that a citizen might be afraid of possible repercussions, such as the disapproval of family members or employers or other citizens, or potential embarrassment. Some may feel free to express their true preference only if their vote is private. It is as if there is a presumption of retaliation. The drawback of secret voting is the risk of behind-the-scenes tampering with the votes.

So a compromise approach is to allow both public and private voting, and let voters choose how to vote, whether by a public affirmation or by a private choice behind a curtained voting booth. To prevent fraud associated with private voting, when a person votes in the booth, there should be an exact hardcopy of their anonymous vote. So there will be two copies of their vote: one recorded by the machine, and a second one that is an exact duplicate of their official vote without, of course, any identifying information about the voter. The duplicate goes to a nonpartisan news media outlet immediately after the official secret vote is cast.

That way, after each vote, there would be two counts: an official count, and a second count for media analysts and journalists, and a discrepancy between the two counts would cast suspicion about what happened, possibly leading to further investigations. The duplicates help prevent behind-the-scenes manipulation of private votes.

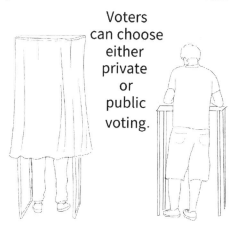

Voters can choose either private or public voting.

The next fix is not a head-scratcher. The problem as pretty much everybody knows is that congresspersons stay in office for decades. They get embedded in these lucrative spots and begin to grow moldy and stale and they stop listening to us. Once in, they'd like to stay there forever, and they have the power to write the rules. The last thing they'd want is term limits.

So we impose term limits.

Representatives serve one two-year term and then they're out. They must wait two years before being eligible to be in Congress again. A system of two years in and two years out is necessary to prevent the ongoing temptation of incumbent politicians to abuse their legislative power to guarantee their reelections.

With a term limit policy of two years in and two years out, there would be no incumbents running for reelection, so elections would be more competitive, benefiting citizens.

Current Representatives

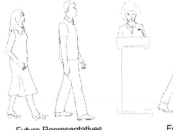

Future Representatives   Former Representatives

The upshot is that every election to Congress has no incumbents and is essentially a competitive contest between newcomers. No party or politician will have the advantage of incumbency. With term limits, voters will have real power to determine what happens in the national legislature. This will lead to higher approval ratings for Congress, which are currently in the single digits to low double digits.

In addition, representatives will be limited to a total of six years in the House. That may encourage them to seek public office elsewhere, perhaps in their state government, or as a senator. We don't want them making a lifelong career as House representatives. We want those positions open to newcomers who will listen to what we want.

We've abandoned congressional districts. With the proposed system, each representative doesn't belong to a particular swath of the map. That's a good change, overall.

So, in New Jersey, where I live, I would not have a single representative exclusive to me, but I could get any of my state's twelve representatives to represent me. Any of them could take my calls, listen to my concerns, possibly answer my questions and possibly advocate for my positions in the legislature.

But these twelve representatives serve all New Jerseyans, not just me. I bet most of the twelve representatives will be too busy to answer my calls or respond to my emails if I try to influence them as a lone individual, so a better way for us to connect with our representatives is through an intermediary.

Let's do some arithmetic. In 2020 the United States population was about 331 million; of these, about 257 million were eighteen years of age and older. Let's assume that 10% of eligible adults would not choose to be citizens for whatever reasons, while acknowledging that this is a rough estimate. If so, there would be about 231 million participating citizens. With only 435 congresspersons, that's one for every 532,000 citizens.

Like I said, congresspersons probably won't listen to me as an individual, or to you either, with 531,999 other constituents to listen to. But congresspersons will listen to a political party, particularly if it has many members. So when we want the government to do something, and if we feel earnestly about something, we find a political party that feels similarly and work with them to get candidates elected.

We connect with our neighbors at citizens' meetings.

We connect with political parties at the citizens' meetings. These will happen three times each year: once in January through April, another from May through August, and a third from September through December. Meeting venues will be close to where we live, at a nearby local gymnasium or auditorium or other public place.

A few things happen during these meetings. First, we declare our current party preference. This is helpful information that will get back to all our representatives as well as the media and the public in general, which will give an up-to-date snapshot of the collective public mind. It says what we want.

Second, we can elect officers to act as go-betweens between us and our representatives. So if we have questions or concerns, a meeting secretary can relay them to our state's representatives, and our representatives can answer questions from previous meetings by relaying them back to these secretaries.

Third, we can check up on our fellow citizens. Are we staying informed? If any citizen feels that they've been treated unfairly by the government, then we could learn about such mistreatment at these meetings, and possibly do something about it. If a fellow citizen fails to show up for these meetings, or fails to keep themselves informed with a paid subscription to a legitimate media source, or who repeatedly fails to declare membership in an official political party, then their commitment can be questioned, which might result in a legal process to strip away their citizenship. It's part of our duty as citizens to check up on each other, and to expose slacker citizens and no-shows, as well as people whose citizenship status fluctuates regularly to avoid their responsibilities as citizens. If our citizenship is called into question, it couldn't be removed without going before a judge and a jury of our peers and having them render a verdict.

Fourth, our representatives might want to inform us about what they're doing. Perhaps there might be a brief video presentation for us to watch. Maybe it will be about some of the challenges and constraints that they're facing. It will help us keep informed about the tradeoffs and compromises they'll inevitably face.

Then it's over. Only a half-hour. We go home. Or we could linger if we wish to address more complex topics or follow up on previous discussions. The half-hour length of these meetings is short enough so that we won't be bored with endless drudgery, but long enough so that we can satisfy our minimal duties as citizens.

But overall, we're there. We are participating in the democratic process. We are acting like real citizens.

In the start-up period, citizens would choose which meeting to attend. There could be many slots available: several times each day, several days each week, daytimes and evenings, throughout the four-month interval. Venues should be big enough to accommodate a fairly large crowd, such as high school gymnasiums or local auditoriums.

Over time, however, we would gravitate toward a particular meeting time and place. It's helpful to build camaraderie if the same group of citizens keeps going to the same meeting. We get to know each other. We can look out for each other.

So as individual citizens, we'd choose a meeting time that's convenient for our schedules. By my rough calculations, if New Jersey designated one hundred venues for these meetings, and offered eight meeting times for each of the five weekdays during the four month interval, and if attendance was distributed randomly, then there would be about a hundred citizens at each meeting. That's a manageable number. States can simply add more venues and more time slots if meetings are too crowded.

Large states like California and Texas would probably have more venues, of course. So would spread-out states like Montana and Wyoming, to accommodate rural citizens. While some states may allow virtual meetings for added convenience, face-to-face meetings are preferred since people could verify that others were participating, and such interactions would make it easier for people to share information, to socialize, and as I said, to look out for each other. Though states will be in charge of choosing meeting places and times, they have an incentive to encourage participation since it will bolster their representation in the House of Representatives.

We've fixed the House of Representatives. But there are other branches to fix.

We've made the House responsive to us. We will have a powerful say in what issues lawmakers discuss and what laws they make. Our representatives are likely to mirror what we think. Their deliberations are likely to be robust. Elections will be competitive without incumbent candidates. In all likelihood, the pernicious influence of money in politics would be lessened dramatically.

However, each incoming batch of representatives will lack experience in government. They're newcomers. They won't know who is who and what is what. Their lack of experience will be particularly evident at the beginning of each two-year term. They will be learning on the job and trying to master the mechanics of lawmaking.

The problem is that we need a strong domestic government to be able to monitor the newly powerful foreign policy department. That means we need federal officials with experience and training and knowledge of how the government works.

This is where the Senate comes in. The Senate will counterbalance the House's lack of experience.

If we impose two-year term limits on the House, we should have no such limits on the Senate. At present, senators serve six-year terms, which is plenty of time to get knowledgeable about government. Further, the current Constitution wisely staggered their terms to avoid a situation in which the entire incoming Senate was inexperienced—every two years, only a third of senators may be up for reelection, so the remaining two thirds will not be neophytes. Currently there are no term limits for senators, and we should keep it this way. The nation benefits when senators have long careers in office. They'll know how things work. They'll know the mechanics of running the domestic side of the federal government.

So, staying true to the handyperson rule, we keep what works. Let's keep the number of senators at one hundred, with two senators per state, with staggered six year terms.

But we fix the flaws.

The first flaw with the Senate is not with their long terms of office but with their function. At present, they're a co-equal branch with the

The House of Representatives and the Senate balance each other for a strong government.

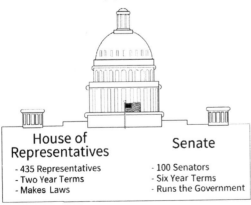

House of Representatives
- 435 Representatives
- Two Year Terms
- Makes Laws

Senate
- 100 Senators
- Six Year Terms
- Runs the Government

House of Representatives. They're half the legislature. They have a powerful impact on what Congress does. They can ignore bills passed by the House. As mentioned previously, since each state has exactly two senators, populous states are underrepresented and rural states are overrepresented, so senators often steer federal aid to states that need it least.

So we change their function from making law to running the government. Senators will manage federal agencies like the Treasury Department, the Internal Revenue Service, the Department of Agriculture, and the Department of Homeland Security. These agencies need experienced managers.

With the current system, since the president appoints people to head various federal agencies, they are tempted to appoint friends or fellow party members, sometimes as a patronage reward for having helped them get elected. So these agencies are sometimes led by unqualified managers who may not know what they're doing and who may be learning on the job.

With the proposed system, however, instead of presidential appointees, senators will be running these agencies. They are more likely to have the skills to be good managers. Senators would shuffle to different agency posts from time to time. The benefit of rotating offices is to prevent corruption if a senator stayed in the same position for too long.

The second flaw with the Senate is how senators are chosen. Currently they're directly elected by the citizens of their state by the winner-take-all arrangement. It would be better to have senators chosen by their state govern-

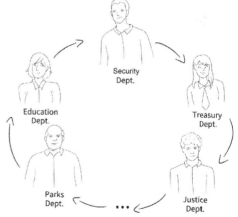

Senators manage executive agencies, and shuffle to new positions every two years.

ments. This is how the Framers set it up. It was changed around 1920 and we should change it back.

There are two reasons.

First, state governments are better positioned to make good choices. They can screen applicants, study candidates' resumes, and debate internally about their qualifications and integrity and managerial skills. Every year their two senators will return to address the state government about what's happening in Washington, so state legislators can see, up close and in person, whether their senators are doing an adequate job. State governments are well positioned to vet their senators and to monitor their performance.

Citizens, in contrast, are not well positioned to choose senators. Since the task of being a senator will shift from making legislation to administering the government, most of us might not be that interested in measuring a candidate's administrative skill. What we're good at is evaluating our own personal situation: are we happy, are we employed, do we have money, do we feel safe, and do we think the government as a whole is doing a good job? We're less willing to sift through resumes. We can still have an indirect influence on our state government's choices by voting in state elections. If journalists identify and expose a corrupt senator, then the public could exert pressure on state legislators to remove him or her.

The second reason is that letting states choose their senators reinforces their connection with the federal government. It gives states a say in what happens in Washington. States can get first-hand information from their own senators. States have skin in the national game. If state officials are unhappy with what happens there, they can do something about it: they can replace their senators. Further, each state should decide how long their senators will serve. Some senators may have long careers there.

Accordingly, with long terms, and with hopefully intelligent oversight from state governments, the Senate would be an important counterweight to the House with its constant influx of inexperienced lawmakers.

Senators would report back to their state governments each year to keep them apprised of what was happening at the federal level. These reports will be staggered so that the senators would not be all away from the government at the same time.

There are enough federal agencies so that all one hundred senators would have plenty of positions to fill. Becoming effective administrators in a complex nation takes time. It will help give the federal government much-needed stability and confidence to counter the newly empowered State Department. They will serve as watchdogs over that department, watching what they do, staying informed.

Now we come to the presidency.

The current arrangement is flawed, as we have noted, with a chief executive with too much power and authority, wearing too many hats. They're the head of the domestic government, the head of foreign policy, and the head of a political party. Yet there are few qualifications for them other than being of a minimum age and having been born in the United States, and of course winning an election. There are no tests for experience. There are no requirements that the president have a working knowledge of national policy or finance or familiarity with the law.

Past presidents have come into the office with varying levels of experience. Some served as senators or state governors. Some were military officers. Few

Presidents have three tough and conflicting responsibilities; it is hard to find a leader who can juggle all three tasks.

were skilled and knowledgeable about foreign affairs. Some presidents were incompetent. A few fraudulent persons slipped into the office. Almost all presidents could be described as learning on the job. By the time they found out what they were doing, they had to leave the position.

Further, some presidential powers are unnecessary and unjustifiable. For example, the president's power to pardon is easily abused, with no checks on who can be pardoned, or how, or why. This can weaken the justice system; if prosecutors believe that their work of getting criminals into jail can be undone with a mere scribble of the pardon pen, then their ardor to work hard can be dampened.

Running a government is hard. There are many variables and contingencies. It takes time to learn what's what. It is not a job for amateurs or neophytes or trainees.

It follows that selecting the leader of the domestic government, one who is entrusted to manage the slew of administrators and officials who run the various departments, is a difficult task. Are we, the public, qualified to choose the president directly? We don't know the particulars of what the job demands. We have little ability to distinguish what particular skills various applicants for the job might have, merely by listening to campaign speeches or watching advertisements or reading endorsements from journalists. We really do not know. We're not in the government, working with officials on a daily basis. It is difficult for us to get a sense of who the best people are. We don't know them on an individual basis so it is hard for us to assess a possible president's people skills.

That's why it is much better for all of us if the selection of the president is not made by direct popular vote, but rather by our representatives at the end of their two-year term. They've been there. They probably have a good idea of what's going on. They've worked with various officials. They know who they are and their capabilities and their values. They're a much better judge of character than we are.

So a much better approach than the direct popular election of the president is to have our representatives, nearing the end of their two-year term, choose one of the senators to be the president for the next two-year term. By limiting the field of candidates to only one hundred senators, it increases the probability that whoever is selected will have managerial experience in the government.

The senator chosen by the House to be president will serve for two years. The president will assign managerial positions to the other senators in the government. Assignments must shift, so each senator cannot remain in the same agency for more than two years.

Since there will be a head of state and a State Department, the president does not need to deal with foreign policy or treaties or diplomacy or statecraft or appointing ambassadors. Rather, the president's job will be to run the domestic government. So whoever becomes president will not need to know the particulars of statecraft.

The president can still be the head of a political party, but with a multiparty system, the problem of partisanship is less likely to infect the government. Since representatives and senators will come from various political parties, a president will have to work with representatives from different parties in order to get legislation passed. It will be easier for officials at the federal level to make decisions about what is best for the country as a whole, and not what is best for their particular political interests.

Each year the president will address Congress about the state of the nation. This is the present arrangement. Further, each month, the president will address the House in a question-and-answer session to discuss current developments. This way the representatives can judge how well the president is doing.

So, in review, citizens elect representatives, and representatives choose one of the senators to be the president. The president is limited to a two-year term, and after the term is over, they cannot be president until another two years have elapsed, for a maximum of three non-consecutive two-year terms.

When the House passes a bill by a majority vote, the president can decide whether to sign it, and if he or she doesn't sign it, the bill will be vetoed. But the House can override a presidential veto with a two-thirds vote. So the president and the representatives can check each other. This is the present arrangement.

Overall, the proposed domestic government will be strong enough to keep a watchful eye over the foreign policy branch as well as have much better prospects of running the government in a competent fashion. It will be less likely to be ravaged by partisan feuding or subject to partisan gridlock. It will be run by people with experience and yet it will be controlled by the people. The House will have the exclusive power of spending. The inexperience of the House is offset by the experience of the Senate.

There is a staggering effect in that the president is chosen by the representatives at the end of their two-year term. The benefit is that representatives will have had two years to see, first-hand and up close, who the best senators are, their qualifications and experience and knowledge of the issues and people skills, and what challenges they would face. So hopefully they will make an informed choice. They are well situated to choose the best president. Their power to select the president also provides a check on the senators in general, so that senators would be predisposed to assisting House members with legislation, as if they were auditioning for the job of president.

The overall result is a unified and competent domestic government. The House mirrors the voting public so the federal government is in tune with the needs of the people. The Senate provides administrative competence and continuity. The president provides overall leadership to the domestic political effort. So the entire domestic branch of the federal government is stronger and better equipped to counterbalance the State Department.

The French philosopher Montesquieu believed in dividing the government according to function. Each branch could do what it does best, while the different branches could check each other. That way, no one branch could get out of control, or get too heady in its authority and power, since the other branches could rein it in. He argued that the legislature should make the laws, the executive should enforce the laws, and the judiciary should interpret the laws. The Framers used this system in their original design and it has worked well to prevent tyranny.

The idea of a good check on a branch is to prevent it from acting excessively or rashly or exerting power beyond its legitimate authority. At the same time, each branch should do what it does best. If the government was like a tree, each branch should keep to its side, not growing so heavy that it would tilt the trunk or interfere with the other branches. If we use the analogy of the mansion, each function is like a wing: the legislative wing, the executive wing, the judicial wing.

Judicial review was intended as a check on the legislature. It enables the Supreme Court to veto an act of Congress by declaring a law to be unconstitutional. The problem is that this check goes too far: it turns justices into super-legislators, corrupts their function from interpreting the law to one of making the law, and it violates the idea that each branch should stick to its basic function.

Judicial review was written into the Constitution with the two words *in equity*, which the Framers understood, and leading members of the Federalist party understood, but that was not clear to the public. There was scant debate during the Constitutional Convention about the role of the judiciary. So when state governments ratified the Constitution, many people didn't understand how much power was being given to the judiciary.

In the current system, nine unelected aging judges can overpower Congress by declaring a law to be unconstitutional.

This turns judges into super-legislators who are unaccountable to the public.

With the current system, with judges able to overturn the law, there is usually a political battle when a seat on the Supreme Court opens up. It turns into a contest between the two parties to see which side will win. Each side tries to guess how a potential judge might vote on pending issues: Will he or she favor abortion? Will the judge be pro-labor or pro-business? There is less focus on the nominee's judicial competence or knowledge of the law or legal temperament or judicial smarts.

It is further complicated by the fact that Supreme Court appointments are for life. The only way for a Supreme Court judge to lose their position is by death or disability or resignation or impeachment. So in some instances, a judge can decide to retire when there is a like-minded member of their own political party occupying the presidency. They can time their retirement to maintain the ideological bent of the court when they should not be able to do so. Many judges get so old, in their eighties and nineties, that their ability to focus and concentrate on sometimes difficult and ambiguous decisions can be hampered by the infirmities of age.

Few other nations give the judiciary such power. Only the United States and a few other nations elevate judges to this level. Most other democratic nations function just fine by keeping judges out of the business of vetoing the legislature.

So the fix here is to keep the number of Supreme Court justices at nine but to remove their power of judicial review. They need to go back to simply interpreting the law and serving as the court of final review, and they must get out of this business of interpreting the Constitution. Further, term limits of perhaps fifteen years is a reasonable rule; that way the court is less likely to be dominated by geriatric justices. Justices should be nominated by the president and approved by the Senate, as in the current system.

In the United States there are two layers of government: the federal layer and individual state governments. So each person is subject to two different governments. For example, I am a citizen of the United States, and I am also a citizen of New Jersey. I pay taxes to the federal treasury and to my state's treasury. Both governments make rules that affect my life: how fast I can drive, how I run my handyman business, and so forth.

This is the system that the Framers established back with the original Constitution back in 1789. It is an excellent system.

It might seem at first glance that having two governments instead of one, affecting every person, might mean there is less freedom overall. There are two governments that can tax us, fine us, and even imprison us.

But the system of dual governments can allow greater freedom. The biggest boost to freedom is that citizens can move to a different state to escape bad or clumsy regulations.

Consider that the task of regulating economic activity is difficult. What should be the rules regarding driving? Should there be a minimum wage? Should handypersons such as myself be licensed? What should be done about abortion?

Problem is, these questions are difficult. Frankly, I don't know the answers. Neither do government officials. Nor economists. Nor experts. There are many variables that play out over time and figuring out how to make rules and regulations is not easy or clear cut. For example, it may be that requiring handypersons to become licensed drives up the cost to homeowners without resulting in any measurable improvements in service, or maybe licensing helps prevent expensive and costly accidents, or maybe the rules regarding licensing are unclear and just waste everybody's time. In short, we don't know. Nobody knows with certainty.

Now if the only government entity able to make rules was the federal government, then it would have to impose a one-size-fits-all rule on handypersons across the country. If it is a good rule, great, but if it's a bad rule, everybody suffers. It is a kind of a hit or miss proposition. Once it makes its rules, it is unlikely to change them because of inertia. A rule could be good initially, but as situations change over time, the rule may no longer be applicable, but we'll still be stuck with it.

But if each state has its own rules about handypersons, then it is possible for handypersons as well as businesses to move to the states that regulate the best. It's like there are fifty concurrent experiments in regulating. I'm not smart enough to set up rules regarding handypersons but I can learn, rather easily, that if I move to Pennsylvania, that I might make more money there or have better clients or be able to hire associates who are better protected against accidents. Maybe Pennsylvania figured out how to regulate handypersons better than New Jersey, through a process of trial and error. But I may not have to move: New Jersey might want to keep handypersons in its state, so there might be pressure on state officials to copy some of Pennsylvania's excellent regulations, if they were perceived as being excellent.

In sum, the competition between states to attract businesses and not lose citizens and tax dollars means that everybody benefits. This interstate jockeying means that the state governments are under pressure to regulate wisely. We are less likely to be subject to an onerous one-size-fits-all rule. This huge freedom to move to a different state protects everybody in a general way from being subject to clumsy regulations, or overly burdensome taxes, or tax filing requirements that are frustrating and complex.

The problem with the current arrangement is that the federal government has usurped too much regulatory authority from the states. Creative interpretations of the Constitution's Commerce Clause have enabled a slew of regulatory agencies to deal with housing, education, national parks, transportation, and so on. Washington is awash in so-called alphabet soup agencies staffed by appointed bureaucrats who try their best to make fair rulings but their record of success has been mixed. It is hard to calculate how much of this federal activity is beneficial and how much is harmful or wasteful.

Perhaps the biggest argument against federal management of the economy is that there are no serious constraints on its power to run things. If it makes a bad ruling, it's hard to identify it and fix it; once a federal rule-making agency gets set up, it's hard to dislodge. It becomes an unthinking advocate for itself to keep getting a bigger budget with more regulatory authority. Since the federal government controls the money supply, it could embark on wasteful policies and simply print more money to cover up its clumsiness.

States, in contrast, are constrained by each other. Since they can't print money, they have to balance their budgets. They can't simply raise taxes to cover up wasteful economic regulations. If states are inept economic managers, then people and businesses will go elsewhere, essentially voting with their feet, and this competitive pressure is likely to keep states working to attract persons and businesses. There is no such brake on the federal government since it is much harder for a person to change countries.

A downside which happens if every state has total regulatory authority is a lack of coordination. If each state had their own peculiar design for speed limit signs on highways, for example, that might confuse drivers. In situations involving interstate affairs, it makes sense to have a level of coordination and consistency in the law.

So the general gist of the fix is to have states regulate as much of their respective economies as they can, since they're closer to the problems, and they're constrained by being unable to print money and by competition from other states. But if a majority of states decide that they would like the federal government to intervene in an area that would benefit from uniform consistency, then they can ask the House to make laws in that area and to set up a federal agency to study the issue and propose solutions. While a federal agency could propose policies, the states would be in charge of implementing and enforcing those policies. Further, the federal agency's authority would be limited to a period of, say, twenty years, after which time the agency would be dissolved, unless a majority of the states again insisted that the agency remain active. It is like a term limit for a federal agency.

With highway signs, for instance, there's clearly a need for nationwide consistency. A majority of states would insist that Congress set up a transportation-related agency, give it power for twenty years, and the agency would suggest consistent designs and formats and rules. If the agency is inept or corrupt or proposes clumsy regulations, then the states could take away its power.

An optimal arrangement would have states regulating as much as they reasonably can, particularly when an issue is internal to the state and unlikely to affect other states. Issues that they should control include healthcare, housing, insurance regulations, licensing, abortion policy, prisons, state taxation policy, and public parks. Issues which they would likely ask for guidance from the federal government include interstate commerce, pollution rules, air travel, and so forth. As much as possible the federal government should avoid interfering in areas where state governments are better suited for regulating, and instead should focus on fighting crime, protecting human rights, simplifying

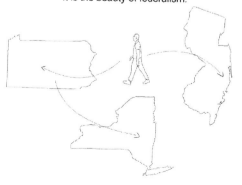

If a state regulates badly, we can "vote with our feet" by moving to a different state.
It is the beauty of federalism.

the tax code, bolstering safety, preparing against natural disasters, and managing the national military.

States should be the only entities managing transfer payments. These happen when lawmakers institute policies that take money from one group of people and give it to another group, such as when money is redistributed from rich people to poor people, from younger workers to older retirees, or from homeowners to homeless people. The transfers happen without work being done, or something of value exchanged; rather they are made since it is believed that it is the right thing to do to rectify an imbalance or inequality.

The risk with any transfer payment is that the recipients of such transfers are, in a sense, bribed. They are getting money without earning it. As citizens, they could vote for political parties that promise to keep this money flowing to them even when they don't really need it. It is an invitation for corruption. At the same time, there are often good reasons for such transfers to take place.

The benefit of enabling states to manage transfer payments, and preventing the federal government from doing so, is to contain possible corruption. Since states are competing with each other to regulate wisely, and to attract citizens and businesses, and since they can't enlarge the money supply, they are pressured to enact sensible transfer payments. It's fine if New Jersey taxes property owners to build homeless shelters if it feels that's the right thing to do, and property owners are fine with such a policy. If the tax levels become unreasonable, people and businesses could move to another state. If New Jersey transfers money from younger people to older people, then as a younger person I may make less money, but be better provided for when I retire. I might like this system and agree to it at various points in my working life. But if the system becomes onerous, I could move to a different state.

There is pressure on New Jersey to behave in a regulatory sense. But there is no such pressure on the federal government. It should stay out of the business of transferring money via programs such as Social

Security or Medicare or Medicaid, since there are few constraints on its activity.

So, recapping, the smart way to divide the tasks, in keeping with the spirit of federalism, is as follows:

- The national government should focus on protecting the nation, preventing violence within the nation, protecting privacy and individual human rights, and settling disputes between the states.
- State governments should regulate business, determine social policy, allow transfer payments, and promote environmental policy. When states feel a need for national consistency, then they can ask the federal government for guidance.

The current Constitution features some checks and balances that work well and others that don't. Since some structures have changed with our proposed revamp, we'll need to rework the system. The purposes are well known: to counterbalance the weakness of one branch with the strength of another, to break up power centers, to prevent abuse and tyranny, and to permit the constitutional system to continue despite changing developments.

Ideally other departments should be able to rein in an out-of-control power center. One way to do this is to give each power center its own sphere of authority, with a separate and clearly defined function, but let other power centers check their authority without taking over their assigned roles.

Accordingly, a basic check with the proposed Constitution is to limit each branch to its assigned sphere of authority. The House will make laws. The Senate will administer the domestic government. The president will coordinate this administration. The Supreme Court will interpret the law and be the final arbiter of domestic cases. International cases will be decided by the State Department's Military Court. The State Department will control foreign policy. Each branch will do what it does best.

A check on the power of the president is similar in terms of

A new system of checks and balances will prevent an abuse of power by any one branch.

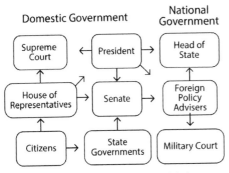

Note: each arrow represents a proposed check

circumscribed authority. The proposed Constitution checks the president's power by limiting their responsibility to overall management of the domestic government. They will still be the head of a political party, but not one of only two powerful political parties, but one of the many parties in a multiparty system. Accordingly, the change from a two-party to a multiparty system will act as a check on presidential partisanship. The president will have to work with a multiparty House and with senators from different parties.

A general check on many branches is term limits. This will prevent House congresspersons from staying in office for decades by abusing the power of incumbency. Term limits will further check the presidency and the Supreme Court. If an inept or abusive congressperson or president gets into office, then the worst that could happen is that they do their damage for only two years, and then they're out. To get back into office, they'd have to again be elected, and most likely officials would be aware of their past incompetence and choose somebody else.

The branches without term limits, specifically the Senate and officials in the State Department, will be heavily checked by other branches. These branches need experienced and competent officials who know what they're doing, and in both instances, term limits do not make sense, because they need time to acquire the knowledge and skills to do their jobs properly. So the checks on their power must be in the form of enabling other officials to fire them. Accordingly, the president can fire any official within the State Department without explanation. So can the Senate with a simple majority vote. But there must be limits on their ability to remove errant State Department officials: specifically, no more than ten officials can be removed within any twelve-month period.

That way, the institution as a whole can keep enough advisers to preserve institutional memory.

There is an internal check within the State Department on the head of state. They serve only at the behest of the State Department advisers who will watch them to make sure that they're doing a competent job. If not, they can be replaced quickly. This is a huge improvement from the current system where an inept or incompetent president can only be removed with difficulty.

Senators can stay in office indefinitely, since they don't have term limits, but their proposed role will shift from being a duplication of the House to being federal administrators in the executive branch. Without this legislative authority, they can not steer federal funds to rural and less populous states, and this change curtails the so-called Senate skew. Their power will be checked by their own state governments, who they will report to each year and who must reappoint them every six years. In addition, the senators themselves can remove an errant senator by a two-thirds majority vote. The House will have a similar power to remove any errant senator with a two-thirds vote.

Another general check is reporting requirements. Most officials will have to make an annual report to officials in other branches. For example, State Department advisers and the head of state will report to the president and Congress. The president will report to the House every month. Senators will report to their state governments every year.

Another check is strengthening the press. In the current system, journalists and newspapers have been struggling financially, with much of their profits eroded by social media companies copying their material without payment. So their role as watchdogs over the government has been weakened. Many people don't subscribe to a legitimate media source. With the proposed Constitution, however, citizens will be required to pay for such subscriptions, so news media outlets will have funds to hire reporters and editors who can work to keep officials honest and to keep everybody informed. The competition between media sources for solid facts and unbiased reporting will help keep them honest—that is, various media sources will check each other. In addition, citizens will help verify that media sources are indeed legitimate and trustworthy, since they can call into question those citizens who subscribe to substandard or biased media sources.

The power of the House is checked as well, since its ability to pass economic regulations is curtailed by the collective action of state governments. If state governments have trouble regulating a specific industry, they can hand over authority to Congress, but even then, their power to regulate interstate commerce has a term limit of twenty years.

The biggest check of all is citizens. That's us. We will be paying attention. We will stay informed about current events. We will know, firsthand and up close, whether our congresspersons are doing a competent job of advancing our interests. Right now, under the current system, most citizens are better described as clueless bystanders who may or may not choose to get involved in any particular issue. Maybe a few get passionate about a particular cause, but it's difficult for them to arouse the rest of us to fix any possible abuse. But in the new arrangement, that shouldn't be a problem. Three times a year, we will meet for a half-hour, and that is when we can inform each other about problems.

In the current arrangement, many politicians seem to be primarily motivated by personal financial gain rather than public service. Many emerge during their tenure much wealthier than when they had entered. Government positions should not be a means toward personal enrichment but rather toward public betterment.

So in the proposed Constitution, there should be limits on an official's total net worth, with the idea being to enable them to be comfortable enough financially to be immune from bribes, and yet not be so wealthy that they have undue influence in the public sphere. So there are caps on the net worth of officials in both the domestic and foreign policy branches of the government. If their net worth exceeds a set limit, then they must pay the excess in taxes to the treasury for the next year. Annual salaries as well as limits on total net worth will be based on the average annual household income for citizens, so if officials would like to increase their salaries and net worth, they'll have to raise the income and wealth of all citizens.

A Renovated Structure

THERE HAVE BEEN ENOUGH FIXES to the basic house of America that it is worthwhile to review the changes so we can analyze the structure as a whole. While many things have been kept, many are new, so let's highlight the changes.

The **State Department** has been moved from being one department within the executive branch to being a separate branch of the federal government. It will control all variables associated with foreign policy: diplomacy, the national military, ambassadors, rules of engagement, treaties, rules guiding Americans who visit foreign countries as well as rules guiding visitors from other nations, immigration, statecraft and long-term planning. Unlike the old structure, it is much less likely to be subject to partisan political considerations. Since it will have the exclusive power to determine foreign policy, it will be accountable to the rest of the government for its actions. With its **head of state,** it can act quickly in a national emergency, and with its one hundred and one **advisers,** it can make long range plans and carry them out. It will have its own judiciary to handle international disputes. The rest of the federal government can control the people but not the policies of the State Department—for example, the president and senators can fire State Department officials but can not tell them what to do. Accordingly, the foreign policy of the nation is much more likely to be coherent and focused, able to adhere to decades-long strategies, less likely to coddle foreign dictators, and more likely to keep the country out of needless and expensive foreign wars.

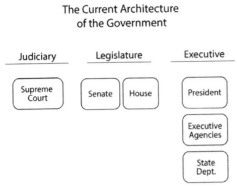

The Current Architecture
of the Government

Judiciary   Legislature   Executive

Supreme Court | Senate | House | President

Executive Agencies

State Dept.

Citizens are empowered. We will no longer be clueless bystanders who can participate or not participate, but rather we would be required as part of our duties to pay attention, to choose a political party, and to monitor other citizens. The shift is from passive citizenship to active citizenship. This change will get to the heart of what's wrong with America, since many of our problems are based on the clueless out-to-lunch nonparticipation of the public. For us, it will be the biggest change affecting our lives, but even then, it will only require a minimal time commitment of a half-hour every four months. As part of the citizenship contract, citizens will protect each other by monitoring our interactions with authorities, so we will not have to rely on guns for self-protection. We will be less inclined to fall into the trap of identity politics, and more inclined to vote based on issues.

Political parties are newly invigorated and stronger. They will have greater power to represent us in the public sphere and to more faithfully mirror the public. There will be a shift from the Coke or Pepsi two-party system to a multiparty system so that there will be more options for us to participate and to be represented. With revised election rules, parties will have greater power to place their candidates on the ballot.

Election rules will eliminate gerrymandering by getting rid of the one representative per fixed geographic district system. The shift is from a winner-take-all system to a party-proportional system within each state.

The **House of Representatives** will continue to have 435 members. With term limits, every congressional race will have no incumbents and will therefore be competitive. This is a huge bonus for us since candidates and political parties will have to listen to what we want when they try to get elected. The pervasive influence of check-writers and lobbyists and influence peddlers will be thwarted substantially. It will give us an important voice in the federal government. Further, the House will be the main legislative body and it will not have to share power with the Senate.

In the past, **state governments** have been sidelined in terms of their influence in the federal government because the Supreme Court has often ruled against their regulatory authority with creative interpretations of the Constitution's Commerce Clause. When state govern-

The Proposed Architecture of the Government

Domestic		National
President	Senate (Executive Agencies)	Head of State
Supreme Court	House of Representatives	Foreign Policy Advisers
Citizens	State Governments	Military Court

ments lost the power to appoint senators in the early twentieth century, their influence was further diminished. The proposed changes re-empower the state governments by restoring their regulatory authority in most matters, and by returning to their legislatures the power to appoint senators. Further, states have the power to determine how their own residents interact with their state governments without federal interference.

The role of **senators** will change from being lawmakers to being administrative managers. They will continue to have six-year terms with no term limits so that their accumulated experience and knowledge can offset the inexperience of the House. Since senators will no longer be in charge of budget bills, this will end the so-called Senate skew that brings greater dollars and resources to less populous rural states.

One senator will be elected at the end of each House's two-year term to be the **president.** He or she will be in charge of the domestic side of the government: policies, law, disaster preparedness, protecting the public, preventing crime, protecting individual human rights, monitoring the State Department, and essentially running the country. Each president will have a two-year term limit, and the maximum they could serve as president would be three two-year nonconsecutive terms.

The **Supreme Court** will be the same except without the power of judicial review. Since the nine justices will no longer be able to nullify a law by declaring it to be unconstitutional, partisan bias and politicking will not characterize their rulings. They will continue to be the court of last resort when it comes to resolving legal matters within the country, but the State Department's Military Court will resolve legal matters between countries. With fifteen-year term limits, the infirmities of old age should be less of an issue.

So, as a brief review, citizens elect representatives who serve for two years and whose job it is to make law. At the end of their term, representatives select from among the senators a president to serve for the following two years.

- People become citizens
- Citizens express their will through political parties
- Representatives make law
- The president oversees the domestic government
- Senators manage the federal government
- The Supreme Court interprets the law
- The State Department manages foreign policy

But the most important change is that we are making people the bedrock of the Constitution. We will no longer be fake citizens. We will have a government of the people, by the people, and for the people.

That's my take. We keep the good stuff. We fix the flaws.

I'm only one guy. Just a handyman. I don't know everything. So there may be a better arrangement. What follows is a tentative Constitution. If the United States has another constitutional convention, it will be good if the new Constitution is pretty close to the one I've proposed or if it solves the problems I've outlined.

America appears strong and solid but there are serious cracks in its foundation. It's time to fix them. Let's think like we're the handypersons having to fix our own house. If nothing is done, America may crumble down fast, deadly, without notice.

So let's fix America.

To signify your support for substantive reform, tie red, white and blue ribbons around trees near you.

A Proposed Constitution

Preamble

WE THE CITIZENS OF THE United States, in order to form a more perfect union, establish justice, ensure domestic tranquility, provide for the common defense, promote the general welfare, and secure the blessings of liberty to ourselves and our posterity, do ordain and establish this Constitution for the United States of America.

Article I – Citizens

Definition. Citizens are members of the body politic of the United States who fulfill the duties and enjoy the privileges of citizenship, and who are recognized as citizens by the government and by fellow citizens, and who recognize the Constitution as the legitimate authority of the United States. Citizenship is a relation between the person and the state that is voluntarily chosen by both, and exists with the consent of the state and fellow citizens. The relationship is characterized by activity and commitment over time.

Eligibility. Persons eligible for citizenship must be at least eighteen years of age. They must be of sound mind, be not substantially dependent on another person, be not substantially dependent on a drug or another addictive substance such that it interferes with their personal autonomy, and be not beholden to a foreign government or a powerful foreign group. Persons must understand the responsibilities and privileges of citizenship. Citizens must have graduated from an accredited high school or have earned an equivalent degree.

Becoming a citizen. To become a citizen, applicants choose citizenship freely and without duress in a public ceremony in which they affirm an oath of loyalty to the nation and to fellow citizens. They commit to supporting individual rights. They sign a copy of the Constitution with at least one witness from the government as well as one witness who is a citizen, in a manner prescribed by Congress.

Responsibilities. Citizens must uphold individual rights, obey the law, pay taxes, vote, attend regularly-held meetings with fellow citizens thrice yearly of at least a half hour each time, keep informed about current events, serve on juries if summoned, subscribe to legitimate news services, and declare membership in a political party. Citizens promise to serve in the armed forces and must fulfill their promise if summoned. Citizens must defend fellow citizens if the government abuses its authority. Citizens visiting foreign nations must follow the guidelines of the State Department.

Pledge. Citizens pledge an oath of loyalty to the nation, to the Constitution, and to each other.

Privileges. Citizens are entitled to equal protection under the law, to due process, and to protections specified by the Bill of Rights.

Meetings. Citizens must attend at least one half-hour citizens' meeting every four-month quadrimester, for at least three times per year. Meetings will be held in shifts at convenient times in venues determined by their state's government, and such meetings shall happen often enough so that the average number of citizens at each meeting is reasonable. Attendance shall be recorded and published. Citizens elect officers including a secretary to submit questions to representatives and to transmit answers from representatives. During a national emergency, the attendance requirement may be waived. At each meeting, citizens must declare their support for a political party, and for an official political party at least half the time. Representatives may submit a brief video presentation that is not to exceed five minutes in length. Advertising and self-promotion and electioneering and other non-public matters shall be prohibited.

Powers. Citizens, assembled, can summon fellow citizens to attend meetings. They can request an explanation from a non-attending citizen about their absence. Citizens can initiate legal proceedings against other citizens for failing to observe the requirements of citizenship. If a citizen is charged with a crime or detained by the government, then other citizens can request an explanation from the government, and the government must comply with such requests in a reasonable manner. Only citizens can hold positions as officers in the federal government.

Questioning lawmakers. Citizens, assembled, can query lawmakers about their past or future choices by submitting questions through their elected secretaries, and lawmakers can query citizens about their preferences and concerns through the secretaries. Each should be responsive to the reasonable requests of the other. At the end of each quadrimester, each state's meeting secretaries and representatives can meet at a time and place determined by state authorities to ask and answer questions.

Non-citizen residents. Persons who live within the nation legally but who are not citizens are non-citizen residents. Persons have the right to choose to be non-citizen residents. All non-citizen residents should be given regular and reasonable opportunities to apply or reapply for citizenship, and Congress shall specify which procedures or tests must be done before a former citizen can be restored to citizenship or a non-citizen can gain citizenship. All rights, privileges, duties, and responsibilities of non-citizens, as well as designations thereof, shall be made by Congress.

Ending citizenship. The relation of citizenship can be dissolved by either the citizen himself or herself, or by the state, or by fellow citizens, only through a legally recognized due process. The relationship can end by two methods. First, a citizen may willingly renounce citizenship. Second, the government or other citizens can present a case to an impartial jury of citizens and they must prove beyond a reasonable doubt that a specific citizen has failed to adhere to the duties of citizenship, or has committed some act or transgression that warrants severing the bond of citizenship. Such transgressions include breaking the law, failing to vote, not attending local meetings, not fulfilling one's military duty if summoned, committing treason, or failing to observe proper guidelines set forth by the State Department when the citizen visits a foreign nation or interacts with a foreign national or a foreign government. Before the bond of citizenship can be legally severed, the courts must follow due process in which the person has the right to contest the severance in a jury trial of fellow citizens.

Article II – The Bill of Rights

First amendment. Congress shall make no law respecting an establishment of religion, or prohibiting the free exercise thereof; or abridging the freedom of speech, or of the press; or the right of the citizens peaceably to assemble, and to petition the government for a redress of grievances.

Second amendment. It shall be the duty of all citizens to protect their fellow citizens if the government becomes abusive or tyrannical or fails to observe due process in its dealings with citizens.

Third amendment. No soldier shall, in time of peace be quartered in any house, without the consent of the owner, but in a manner to be prescribed by law.

Fourth amendment. The right of the people to be secure in their persons, houses, papers, and effects, against unreasonable searches and seizures, shall not be violated, and no warrants shall issue, but upon probable cause, supported by oath or affirmation, and particularly describing the place to be searched, and the persons or things to be seized.

Fifth amendment. No citizen shall be held to answer for a capital, or otherwise infamous crime, unless on a presentment or indictment of a grand jury, except in cases arising in the land or naval forces, or in the militia, when in actual service in time of war or public danger; nor shall any citizen be subject for the same offense to be twice put in jeopardy of life or limb; nor shall be compelled in any criminal case to be a witness against himself or herself, nor be deprived of life, liberty, or property, without due process of law; nor shall private property be taken for public use, without just compensation.

Sixth amendment. In all criminal prosecutions, the accused shall enjoy the right to a speedy and public trial, by an impartial jury of the state and district wherein the crime shall have been committed, which district shall have been previously ascertained by law, and to be informed of the nature and cause of the accusation; to be confronted with the witnesses against them; to have compulsory process for obtaining witnesses in their favor, and to have the assistance of counsel for their defense.

Seventh amendment. In suits at common law, where the value in controversy shall exceed a minimum amount set by law, the right of trial by jury shall be preserved, and no fact tried by a jury, shall be otherwise re-examined in any court of the United States, than according to the rules of the common law.

Eighth amendment. Excessive bail shall not be required, nor excessive fines imposed, nor cruel and unusual punishments inflicted.

Ninth amendment. The enumeration in the Constitution, of certain rights, shall not be construed to deny or disparage others retained by the citizens.

Tenth amendment. The powers not delegated to the United States by the Constitution, nor prohibited by it to the states, are reserved to the states respectively, or to the citizens.

Right of privacy. Citizens have a right of privacy. It is the duty of Congress to specify which information shall be considered to be private and make rules governing publicly-held private information. Citizens have a right to view their publicly held private information and to determine which parties or institutions have this information. Keepers of private information, including the government, have a duty to keep private information private, and may be held liable for breaches of privacy.

Government obligation. Government is required to treat all citizens fairly and to observe all rules regarding citizenship.

Nondiscrimination clause. Government must not discriminate against citizens based on their religious creed, skin color, race, ethnicity, sex, gender, sexual orientation, or other involuntary personal attributes.

Press access. Journalists have a right to access counts of party preferences, voting records, deliberations of legislators, and other discussions of policy by public officials, with the exception of matters involving foreign policy and national security.

Article III – Political Parties

Definition. A political party is a group of citizens with a common political agenda.

Legitimacy. A political party is legitimate if its agenda is consistent with the basic norms of a democratic republic, including a respect for free and fair elections, majority rule, voting, individual human rights, national self-determination, and one person one vote.

Party names. Political parties shall have a specific name composed of not more than thirty letters of the alphabet, including spaces, precisely spelled.

Citizen declaration. At the end of every citizens' meeting, each citizen shall declare their choice of a political party, and every preference shall be published and recorded. Citizens may choose only one party.

Party formation. If a party achieves two percent of the declared citizen preferences on any one day, of all citizens nationwide, then it shall be designated as an official political party, and it shall keep such a designation for the following twenty-four months. If an official party fails to maintain two percent of declarations during a twenty-four month interval, its official designation shall be removed.

Party leadership. An official political party can elect leaders, designate candidates for office, and the names of these candidates shall be posted publicly.

Party platform. An official political party must publish a platform of its positions in a written statement of not more than five hundred characters, including spaces. This platform will be in effect for a period of at least twelve months, after which time it can be amended or changed, which begins a new period of twelve months. It can publish secondary explanations of its positions in addition, at its discretion.

Party standing. For an official party to remain in good standing, its members must respect the democratic-republican principles of reasoned argument, respect for facts, individual rights, toleration of opposing views, majority rule, voting, and the peaceful transfer of power. It must neither espouse violence nor willfully distort public information nor advocate the violent overthrow of the legitimately elected government. If an official party's leaders or candidates fail to meet these standards, then its standing can be challenged by the House of Representatives, and removed as an official party with the consent of at least three-fourths of the representatives.

Article IV – The House of Representatives

Organization. All legislative powers herein granted shall be vested in the House of Representatives.

Frequency of assembly. The House of Representatives shall assemble at least once every month.

Voting. The House shall be the judge of the elections, returns and qualifications of its members, and a majority shall constitute a quorum to do business; but a smaller number may adjourn from day to day, and may be authorized to compel the attendance of absent members, in such manner, and under such penalties as the House may provide.

Rules. The House may determine the rules of its proceedings, punish its members for disorderly behavior, and, with the concurrence of two-thirds, expel a member.

Record keeping. Each House shall keep a journal of its proceedings, and from time to time publish the same, excepting such parts as may in their judgment require secrecy; and the yeas and nays of the members on any question shall be recorded and published.

Compensation. The representatives shall receive compensation for their services, to be ascertained by law, and paid out of the treasury of the United States.

Privilege. They shall in all cases, except treason, felony, and breach of the peace, be privileged from arrest during their attendance at their session, and in going to and returning from the same.

No double offices. No representative shall, during the time for which they were elected, be appointed to any civil office under the authority of the United States, which shall have been created, or the emoluments whereof shall have been increased during such time; and no person holding any other office under the United States, shall be a member of the House during their continuance in office.

Legislative transparency. The House must make public its decisions, allocations of funds, summaries of discussions, voting records on bills, and other matters with the exception of matters relating to national security, defense, or other foreign policy issues.

The powers of the House of Representatives include ...

Taxation. To lay and collect taxes, duties, imposts, and excises.

Defense. To pay the debts and provide for the common defense and general welfare of the United States; but all duties, imposts and excises shall be uniform throughout the United States.

Borrowing. To borrow money on the credit of the United States.

Minting money. To coin money, regulate the value thereof, and of foreign coin, and fix the standard of weights and measures.

Punish counterfeiters. To provide for the punishment of counterfeiting the securities and current coin of the United States.

Post offices. To establish post offices and post roads.

Stance. To declare either war or peace, and to signify the nation's official stance with a flag designated for that purpose.

Patents and copyrights. To promote the progress of science and useful arts, by securing for limited times to authors and inventors the exclusive right to their respective writings and discoveries.

Lesser courts. To constitute tribunals inferior to the Supreme Court.

Funds for the national military. To provide monies to support all national military forces, including armies, navies, air forces, marines, space forces, command forces, and supporting personnel.

Military rules. To make rules for the regulation of the militia and the national guard forces.

Summoning militia. To provide for calling forth the militia to execute the laws of the union, suppress insurrections, prevent tyranny, and repel invasions in the event that foreign armies are within the borders of the United States.

Organizing the militia. To provide for organizing, arming, and disciplining the militia, and for governing such part of them as may be employed in the service of the United States, reserving to the states respectively, the appointment of the officers, and the authority of training the militia according to the discipline prescribed by Congress.

Necessary and proper clause. To make all laws which shall be necessary and proper for carrying into execution the foregoing powers, and all other powers vested by this Constitution in the government of the United States, or in any department or officer thereof.

Writ of habeas corpus. The privilege of the writ of habeas corpus shall not be suspended, unless in cases of rebellion or invasion when public safety may require it.

Deficit spending. During times without war or disaster or environmental emergency, if the national spending exceeds the gross domestic product, for the most recent year, then each representative must explain the excess to their own state's legislature, and receive a vote of confidence from the same, and, lacking this, then the representative must vacate their seat in the legislature.

Restrictions. No bill of attainder or ex post facto law shall be passed.

Taxation provision. No capitation or other direct tax shall be laid, unless in proportion to the census or enumeration herein before directed to be taken.

Export taxes. No tax or duty shall be laid on articles exported between states.

No preferences. No preference shall be given by any regulation of commerce or revenue to the ports of one state over those of another; nor shall vessels bound to, or from, one state, be obliged to enter, clear, or pay duties in another.

Appropriations and accountability. No money shall be drawn from the treasury, but in consequence of appropriations made by law; and a regular statement and account of the receipts and expenditures of all public money shall be published from time to time.

No titles. No title of nobility shall be granted by the United States: and no person holding any office of profit or trust under them, shall, without the consent of the Congress, accept of any present, emolument, office, or title, of any kind whatever, from any king, prince, or foreign state.

Simplicity of taxes. Federal tax rules must be straightforward and not overly complex.

Financial disclosures. House representatives must make full and regular disclosures of their finances to the public, including property owned, income, bank accounts, business interests, rents, royalties, and so forth.

Eligibility. Each candidate for election to the House of Representatives must be a citizen of the United States, and belong to a political party which is official and legitimate.

Before the election. At least one month before each election, each official party will publish its platform and a list of its candidates in the rank order of preference. A nationwide poll of party preferences, taken one month before each election, shall determine a party's position on the ballot; accordingly, the most popular party will get the top position, the second-most popular party, a position below the first one, and so on, until all official parties are listed on the ballot. Each state shall determine the places and times and manner of these elections.

Time of election. Elections shall happen during the first week of November of every second year.

Manner of election. Citizens vote in person. If a citizen chooses to vote privately in a booth, there must be one and only one exact copy of their vote printed, without their name or other identifying information, which shows their vote, which shall be given to a state-approved polling organization immediately after the citizen has finished their private vote; if a citizen chooses to vote publicly, their choice is published, and there is no such requirement for a matching duplicate. Each citizen votes for one and only one political party. On their journey to and from the polling venue, citizens must not be harassed or intimidated or subject to partisan appeals or electioneering.

Tabulating the results. State officials count and publish the vote totals for their state. The proportion of votes for each party within each state determines how many House seats each party gets; for example, if there are twenty seats allotted to a particular state based on the most recent national census of citizens, and if a particular political party wins 40% of the vote within that state, then that party is entitled to eight seats. The political party fills the winning seats with its candidates in the exact order of their earlier published order of precedence. If there are not enough candidates to fill a party's allotted seats, then candidates from other parties can be selected at the discretion of the state's governor. If a representative dies or resigns or is otherwise unable to fulfill their two-year term, replacements can be filled by the party to serve out the remainder of their term, with other candidates from the ballot, based on the earlier published order of preference, and if the list of available replacement candidates has been exhausted, then the governor of the state can fill the empty slots as they choose.

No fixed districts. All representatives from a state shall represent all citizens of that state.

Body. The House of Representatives shall be composed of 435 members chosen every second year by the people of the several states and the District of Columbia. Their number from each state will be based on an actual enumeration made every ten years, and this information from this census shall be used to apportion the number of representatives as equally as possible among the several states and the District of Columbia, with the provision that each state shall have at least one representative.

Length of service. Members serve two years. Every two-year term must be followed by at least a two-year absence from the House of Representatives. No member may serve more than a total of six years in the House.

Leadership. The House of Representatives shall choose their speaker and other officers.

House voting. Each representative shall have one vote in the legislature.

House impeachment power. The House shall have the power to impeach and try any officer in the federal government including the senators, head of state, foreign policy advisers, Supreme Court justices, or other officials in the federal government. To begin an impeachment case requires a vote of at least half of the House members, and to convict an official requires a vote of at least three-fourths of House members. When sitting for that purpose, representatives shall be on oath or affirmation.

Judgment in cases of impeachment shall not extend further than to removal from office, and disqualification to hold and enjoy any office of honor, trust, or profit under the United States; but the party convicted shall nevertheless be liable and subject to indictment, trial, judgment, and punishment, according to law. But the House can not remove more than ten State Department advisers in any twelve-month period.

Power to determine treason. The House has the power to determine treason against the United States, which shall consist only in levying war against them, or in adhering to their enemies, giving them aid and comfort; no person shall be convicted of treason unless on the testimony of two witnesses to the same overt act, or on confession in open court. The House shall have power to declare the punishment of treason, but no attainder of treason shall work corruption of blood, or forfeiture except during the life of the person attainted.

The no-confidence check. The House can remove the president by a three-fourths vote of no confidence, in which case the president resumes their role as a senator, and the House by a majority vote must elect another senator to be the president within seven days of the ouster. The House can conduct an ouster of the president only twice during their two-year term of office.

Power of the purse. The House will have authority on federal expenditures. For a bill to become law, the president must sign it, and then it becomes a law. If unsigned, it is vetoed, but the House by at least a three-fourths vote can override the president's veto, and then it becomes a law.

Salary. Representatives shall be paid an annual salary out of the United States Treasury that is equal to double the amount of the average annual household income for the most recent year. For example, if the average is $75,000, then their salary will be $150,000.

Article V – The Senate

Qualifications for office. Senators must have served for at least two years in the House of Representatives or in a state legislature or as a state governor. They must have received training in the law. They must be a citizen of the state that they represent.

Manner of election. Senators shall be chosen by each state government.

Staggered terms. Immediately after they shall be assembled in consequence of the first election, they shall be divided as equally as may be into three classes. The seats of the senators of the first class shall be vacated at the expiration of the second year, of the second class at the expiration of the fourth year, and of the third class at the expiration of the sixth year, so that one third may be chosen every second year; and if vacancies happen by resignation, or otherwise, during the recess of the legislature of any state, the executive thereof may make temporary appointments until the next meeting of the state legislature, which shall then fill such vacancies.

Term of office. The term of office is six years. After six years, their appointment must be renewed by their state government, and if not, then the state government must appoint a new senator from their state.

Two senators per state. Each state shall have exactly two senators.

Choosing foreign policy advisers. The Senate shall nominate advisers for the State Department when positions open up. Once nominated, nominees must be approved by at least three-fourths of the House of Representatives.

Removing foreign policy advisers. The Senate can dismiss particular foreign policy advisers with the concurrence of at least two-thirds of its members. But in any particular twelve-month period, no more than ten advisers in total can be removed by the Senate or the House or the president.

Confirmations. The Senate shall hear cases of pardons suggested by the head of state. At least a two-thirds vote is required for a pardon to be approved.

Duties. Senators administer the government. Their particular roles in the executive branch are chosen by the president. In addition, they serve as advisers to the House on matters of public policy. They monitor the activity of the State Department but they shall not make foreign policy decisions.

Reporting. Once each year, on different days, one at a time, senators shall report in person back to their states on the activity of the national government. In addition, senators may be summoned from time to time by their state governments to answer questions posed by state officials, provided that such meetings do not impede national policymaking.

Article VI – The President
Office. The executive power shall be vested in the office of president of the United States of America.

Requirements. The president must be a member of the Senate.

Reporting exemption. The president is exempt from making an annual in-person report to their state government.

Term. Presidents shall serve for two years, and after serving, they must not be president for the next two years, and after that, they may again be president, and so on, for a maximum of three two-year terms in office.

Election. The president shall be elected by the House of Representatives in the first week of December near the end of each two-year term of the House. The chosen senator becomes president for the succeeding two years.

Removal from office. In case of the president's death, resignation, or permanent inability to discharge the powers and duties of their office, the House with a majority vote shall elect another senator to act as president. If the president is unable to perform their duties for a limited time, then the House shall select another senator to serve as the temporary president until the period of disability is over. Each month the president may continue in office provided there is not a vote of no confidence by three-fourths of the House of Representatives; if there is such a vote, then the president is removed from the presidency and returned to their position in the Senate. If the House decides to impeach the president, impeachment proceedings begin with a majority vote, and then conviction requires a three-fourths vote, and then the president must resign their position both as president and as senator.

Compensation. The president shall, at stated times, receive for their services a compensation that shall neither be increased nor diminished during the period for which they shall have been elected, and they shall not receive within that period any other emolument from the United States or other nation.

Powers. The president shall take care that the laws be faithfully executed. They shall manage the executive operations of the domestic national government, including the treasury, Attorney General, various regulatory agencies, and others that enact and enforce the laws of the United States. They shall be in charge of domestic security including crime prevention, counterterrorism, and public welfare. They shall choose senators to administer the various departments of the domestic government. The president may, on extraordinary occasions, convene the House of

Representatives. The president shall be commander-in-chief of the national guard forces of the states. The president shall command the security forces for all public officials in both the domestic and foreign policy branches of the federal government. The president can fire the head of state without explanation. The president can fire up to ten State Department advisers in any twelve-month period.

Nominating justices. When a position opens up, the president shall nominate justices of the Supreme Court, subject to approval by a majority vote of the House of Representatives.

Restrictions. The president's sphere of authority is limited to domestic matters. They shall not interfere with making or executing foreign policy with the exception of monitoring the officials in the State Department.

Reporting. Each month, at a time scheduled by law, the president must appear before the House to answer questions in a half-hour session broadcast to the public. Each year, the president must make a state of the union speech to the Congress that is broadcast to the public.

Article VII – The Supreme Court

Body. The judicial power of the United States shall be vested in one Supreme Court, and in such inferior courts as the Congress may from time to time ordain and establish. The judges, both of the supreme and inferior courts, shall hold their offices during good behavior, and shall, at stated times, receive for their services a compensation, which shall not be diminished during their continuance in office.

Number. The Supreme Court shall have nine justices.

Length of service. Justices can serve up to fifteen years, at which time they must resign, and they can not be reappointed.

Appointment. Justices shall be nominated by the president, and confirmed by the Senate by a majority vote.

Eligibility. Justices must have at least ten years of substantive experience as lawyers or judges or academics or legal scholars.

Leadership. The justices shall elect one of their number to be Chief Justice, who shall serve provided there is consent among the members, and they shall assign judges to write opinions.

Scope of authority. The judicial power shall extend to all domestic cases, in law and equity, arising under this Constitution, the laws of the United States, or which shall be made, under their authority, in relation to domestic matters, and to all controversies between (1) two or more states (2) between a state and citizens of another state or (3) between citizens of different states or (4) between citizens of the same state claiming lands under grants of different states. The trial of all crimes, except in cases of impeachment, shall be by jury; and such trial shall be held in the state where the said crimes shall have been committed; but when not committed within any state, the trial shall be at such place or places as the Congress may by law have directed. The court shall not nullify acts of the legislature.

Article VIII – The State Department

Scope of authority. The State Department manages foreign policy. It has authority for all statecraft, including relations with foreign nations and foreign individuals, immigration, treaties, ambassadors, foreign aid programs, and espionage. Its rules govern conduct between citizens who travel to foreign nations and foreigners who travel within the nation. It shall have the power to establish a uniform rule of naturalization. The sole exception is that it does not have the power to declare war or peace. Its officials serve at the behest of Congress and the president. It is fully accountable to the domestic government for all of its actions. It has a duty to inform Congress and the president of major developments in foreign affairs.

Departments. It shall have three branches: the foreign policy advisers, the head of state, and the Military Court.

Section 1. Foreign policy advisers

Body. Foreign policy advisers shall number one hundred and one.

Qualifications. Candidates, when appointed, must be younger than forty years of age, with the exception being when the Constitution is ratified, in which case fifty advisers can be chosen regardless of age. Upon appointment, advisers shall renounce their membership in any particular political party.

Appointments. Advisers are nominated by the Senate and confirmed by the House of Representatives with a three-fourths vote.

Length of term. Officials serve as long as they are able, or until they resign, die, succumb to illness, or are removed from office.

Vacancies. When a vacancy happens such that the number of foreign policy advisers is less than one hundred and one, then the Senate shall appoint another adviser to be confirmed by at least three-quarters of the House of Representatives. If a position remains vacant for longer than three months, then the president may nominate a replacement, to be confirmed by the Senate with a majority vote.

Powers and duties. The State Department shall make foreign policy. It shall make treaties with other nations and powers. It shall make rules relating to immigration or relating to visits by citizens abroad or by foreigners visiting. It shall regulate commerce with foreign nations. It shall define and punish piracies and felonies committed on the high seas and in space, and offenses against the law of nations. It shall grant letters of marque and reprisal. It shall make rules concerning captures on land

and water and air and space. It shall construct forts, magazines, arsenals, dockyards, and other needful buildings. It shall organize and lead armies.

Salary. Advisers shall be paid an annual income from the treasury of twenty times the average annual household income of citizens. For example, if the average is $75,000, an adviser's annual salary shall be $1,500,000.

Role within the department. The advisers appoint and dismiss the head of state. Advisers craft foreign policy.

Reporting. Three officers, chosen by the head of state, must report in person to the House of Representatives each quarter, for at least an hour in duration, about the state of the nation and its standing in the world community. In addition, individual advisers can be chosen by the House of Representatives, or by the Senate, or by the president, to report on the activity of the State Department, in public or private, as needed, from time to time.

Removal. Advisers can be removed from their position by the president or by a majority vote of the House of Representatives, with the proviso being that no more than ten advisers in total can be removed in any given twelve-month period by any set of officials in the domestic branch of the government.

Section 2. The head of state

Eligibility. Almost all citizens are eligible except advisers of the State Department, senators and representatives, and the president.

Election. The head of state is chosen by the foreign policy advisers, and must be confirmed by the Senate with a majority vote. If a period of one week elapses without an appointment of a head of state, then the Senate will elect a head of state with a majority vote.

Term. The head of state can serve as long as they are able.

Removal. The head of state serves only with the approval of the foreign policy advisers, who can remove them without explanation at any time. In addition, the president can remove the head of state without explanation.

Reporting. The head of state shall report directly, in person, to the foreign policy advisers, as needed. During peacetime, they must report in person to the Senate at least once every three months.

Powers and duties. The head of state shall be the commander-in-chief of the national armies, and be in charge of espionage agencies, ambassadors, and all staff and personnel related to these functions. They shall make all military appointments. They shall receive foreign leaders, including foreign heads of State, ambassadors, and others at their discretion. They can recommend pardons of particular persons to the Senate only if their particular cases involve foreign affairs, and such pardons will be in effect if at least two thirds of the Senate agrees.

Salary. The head of state shall be paid an annual income from the treasury of thirty times the average annual household income of citizens. For example, if the average is $75,000, the head of state's annual salary shall be $2,250,000.

Section 3. The Military Court

Body. The Military Court shall consist of eleven justices.

Election. Justices will be appointed by the foreign policy advisers.

Length of term. They shall serve for terms up to thirty years.

Qualifications. Each justice must be a lawyer with experience handling military or international cases.

Jurisdiction. The Military Court shall judge all matters relating to foreign policy, including treaties, and acts by citizens or soldiers abroad or by foreigners in the United States. Its judicial power shall extend to: all treaties made, or which shall be made, under the authority of the State Department; to all cases affecting ambassadors, other foreign policy officials and consuls; to all cases of admiralty and maritime jurisdiction; to international controversies to which the United States shall be a party; to controversies between a state or the citizens thereof, and foreign states, citizens, or subjects; to cases involving military discipline of the national armies, or actions by soldiers or officers thereof.

Duties. The court serves as counselors to the advisers on matters of law and treaties. They maintain records of treaties and obligations and international commitments. The justices serve only with the continued approval of the advisers.

Clarity of rules. It is the responsibility of the Military Court to make summaries of its rules accessible and clear to persons who might be affected by such rules, as well as the likely consequences for persons who violate those rules. It must publish a guideline to specify proper behavior for citizens and non-citizen residents who travel to foreign countries.

No retroactive laws. No ex post facto ruling shall be made.

Article IX – State Governments

Scope of regulation. State governments shall have full authority to manage all domestic issues within their state, including the regulation of commerce as well as rules regarding business, education, the professions, health care, licensing, insurance, taxation, abortion policy, and transportation. As much as possible, authority to make and administer rules should be passed down to governments at the county, city, and village levels.

Clarity of rules. States must make their particular rules clear and accessible in summary form to neighboring states, businesses, employers, workers and visitors.

Regulatory assistance from Congress. If a majority of state governments believe that a specific industry or commercial sector cannot be effectively regulated by the various states and that uniform nationwide regulation would be beneficial, then they can request that the Congress intervene and regulate the specific industry or sector for a period of twenty years, and all states must abide by the congressional plan, although enforcement of such congressionally made rules must be managed by the states themselves. After twenty years have passed, the states must either renew the Congressional regulatory authority or else the regulatory authority returns to the states.

Full faith and credit. Full faith and credit shall be given in each state to the public acts, records, and judicial proceedings of every other state. Congress may by general laws prescribe the manner in which such acts, records and proceedings shall be proved, and the effect thereof.

Fugitives. A person charged in any state with treason, felony, or other crime, who shall flee from justice, and be found in another state, shall on demand of the executive authority of the state from which they fled, be delivered up, to be removed to the state having jurisdiction of the crime.

Restrictions. No state shall enter into any treaty, alliance, or confederation; grant letters of marque and reprisal; coin money; emit bills of credit; pass any bill of attainder, ex post facto law, or law impairing the obligation of contracts; or grant any title of nobility. No state shall, without the consent of the Congress, lay any imposts or duties on imports or exports, except what may be absolutely necessary for executing its inspection laws; and the net produce of all duties and imposts, laid by any state on imports or exports, shall be for the use of the treasury of the United States; and all such laws shall be subject to the revision and control of the Congress. No state shall, without the consent of Congress, lay any duty of tonnage, keep troops, or ships of war in time of peace, enter into any agreement or compact with another state, or with a foreign power, or engage in war, unless actually invaded, or in such imminent danger as will not admit of delay.

Districting. States shall specify venues and schedules for citizens' meetings, for the purpose of facilitating such interactions in a fair and efficient manner.

State citizenship. States have full authority to specify rules regarding citizenship in their state, with the exception being that states can not offer state citizenship to persons who are not citizens of the United States. Persons can not be state-citizens of two states, but must choose citizenship in only one particular state; in matters where state citizenship is undecided or disputed or unclear, then the matter will be decided by Congress.

Protection. The United States shall guarantee to every state in this union a republican form of government, and shall protect each of them against invasion; and on application of the legislature, or of the executive (when the legislature cannot be convened), against domestic violence.

Article X – Other Issues
Oath of office. The senators and representatives before mentioned, and the members of the several state legislatures, and all executive and judicial officers, including officers of the State Department, both of the

United States and of the several states, shall be bound by oath or affirmation, to support this Constitution, and must make this pledge in a public place before assuming their official duties: "I do solemnly affirm that I will, to the best of my ability, preserve, protect and defend the Constitution of the United States."

No religious tests. No religious test shall ever be required as a qualification to any office or public trust under the United States.

Financial transparency. The finances of every federal official, including the president, senators, representatives, Supreme Court justices, Military Court justices, State Department advisers and the head of state, must be published, including their salary, assets, net worth, financial transactions, tax returns, stock and real estate holdings, gifts, debts, and rents and royalties. Efforts to conceal wealth and income through intermediaries are prohibited. Officers shall neither have income from foreign sources or be in debt to any foreign persons or firms, widely construed.

Wealth limit. The limit of an official's total net worth, based on properties and businesses owned, cash, stocks and bonds, patents and copyrights, and all other things owned and kept of value, shall not exceed two hundred times the average annual household income of citizens nationwide for the most recent year. No senator, no representative, no president, no State Department adviser, no head of state, and no justices in the Supreme Court or the Military Court shall have a total net worth exceeding that amount, and if their wealth exceeds that total, then the excess must be paid to the United States Treasury for the next taxable year. For example, if the annual average household income for the most recent year is $75,000, then the limit on an official's wealth is $15 million, and if an official's wealth is $20 million, then they shall owe $5 million as part of their next annual tax payment.

Militia versus national military. The militia shall be limited to defending the homeland, maintaining domestic peace, and responding to natural and manmade disasters. The national military shall be limited to actions overseas and in other countries, such as protecting vital interests, securing sea lanes and airspace, assisting allies, and, if necessary, prosecuting wars. The militia will be led by the president; the national military will be led by the head of state.

New states. New states may be admitted by Congress into this union; but no new state shall be formed or erected within the jurisdiction of any other state; nor any state be formed by the junction of two or more states, or parts of states, without the consent of the legislatures of the states concerned as well as of the Congress.

Territories. Congress shall have power to dispose of and make all needful rules and regulations respecting the territory or other property belonging to the United States; and nothing in this Constitution shall be so construed as to prejudice any claims of the United States, or of any particular state.

Amendments. The Congress, whenever two-thirds of both houses shall deem it necessary, shall propose amendments to this Constitution, or, on the application of the legislatures of two-thirds of the several states, shall call a convention for proposing amendments, which, in either case, shall be valid to all intents and purposes, as part of this Constitution, when ratified by the legislatures of three-fourths of the several states, or by conventions in three-fourths thereof, as the one or the other mode of ratification may be proposed by the Congress; provided that no state, without its consent, shall be deprived of its equal suffrage in the Senate.

Supreme law. This Constitution, and the laws of the United States which shall be made in pursuance thereof; and all treaties made, or which shall be made, under the authority of the United States, shall be the supreme law of the land; and the judges in every state shall be bound thereby, any thing in the Constitution or laws of any state to the contrary notwithstanding.

Ratification. The ratification of the conventions of thirty-five of the fifty states shall be sufficient for the establishment of this Constitution between the states so ratifying the same.

Initial selection of advisers. Upon ratification of this Constitution, the Senate may select the first fifty foreign policy advisers regardless of age, but after that, shall choose candidates who are younger than forty years of age.

Term limit for this Constitution. If this Constitution is ratified, then it will be in effect for the next one hundred years, after which time another constitutional convention will be convened to assess its viability and, if necessary, to propose changes and craft a new constitution.

Made in USA - Crawfordsville, IN
77110_9798784524423
08.23.2022 0914